The Best Summer E

A Parents' Guid

·······································

Joan M. Bergstr

EVANS
CHILD
1703 O
EVANS

Tricycle Press
Berkeley, California

9.95

MAY 25 2001

TRICYCLE PRESS
P.O. Box 7123
Berkeley, California 94707

Cover design by Nancy Austin
Text design by Tasha Hall

Cover photographs copyright © 1995 by Miriam de Uriarte,
director and founder, Berkeley Child Art Institute, a non-
profit center which seeks to advance children's creative
learning and development. Berkeley, California.

Library of Congress Cataloging-in-Publication Data
Bergstrom, Joan M.
The best summer ever : a parents guide / Joan M. Bergstrom.
     p. cm.
Includes index.
ISBN 1-883672-22-8
1. Child rearing. 2. Parenting. 3. Family recreation.
I. Title
HQ769.B5182 1995
649'.5—dc20   94-42376
                                                   CIP

First Tricycle Press printing, 1995
Manufactured in Canada
2 3 4 5 6 7 8 — 00 99 98

Contents

· · · · · · · · · · · · · · ·

Thanks and More Thanks

With this second edition, children's use of their out-of-school time, especially during the summer, continues to be an unsubsiding issue in society. Heartfelt, insightful, creative, and innovative solutions have come from a very diverse and talented group of people. Children of all ages, parents, grandparents, sitters, educators, community recreation leaders, camp counselors, journalists, and policy makers have offered to share their day-to-day experiences, feedback, and expertise with me over the years.

There are many people who helped to prepare this book and played a very central and important editorial role. Jean Heifetz assisted to shape the book, spending hours cutting, pasting, and rewording. Barbara Fuller was a superb editor and continued to bring the book to fruition. Both Jean and Barbara were always ready with innovative insights and creative ways to consider or reconsider the presentation of an idea. In the very early stages of the writing, Patricia Gagnon organized the manuscript through her careful attention, writing, and ideas. She also spent much time engaged in conversations with parents.

Both the first and second editions would not have been possible without the hard, resourceful, and determined work of Judy Ceven. Judy was always willing to research the smallest detail, remained calm, and had a sense of determination that, indeed, "we'll make the deadlines and do it perfectly." Thank you to Emily Lentz who also attended to the details while putting together the resources list. Emily is always optimistic and good-humored. Jennifer Ceven assisted to make some of our lists more user-friendly, and often would say, "Joan, did you ever think of that?"

Thanks and many thanks to the team at Tricycle Press. Nicole Geiger and George Young gave very, very generously of themselves. Nicole Geiger spent endless amounts of time to create a friendly and inviting book for parents (I hope we have done that). I always had the sense that Nicole would come up with the right solution to almost any problem or situation presented. Thanks to a great team of editors and a company that is a sheer delight for an author to be associated with over many years. George Young continues to be one of the most patient and talented people I know. His keen questions and conversations always help me to articulate what I know.

With this second edition, I continue to think about this book as a tasty, rich, and textured soup. Many adults and children contributed to give it exciting ingredients, textures, spices, and variations. Thanks again to the extraordinary efforts of everyone who helped, cheered, and made suggestions for the book.

JOAN M. BERGSTROM
January, 1998

Preface

· · · · · · · · · · · · · · · · ·

Summer. For most children, it means at least three months of freedom after nine long months of school. Many see it as a time to do absolutely nothing. This huge block of unstructured time can be as overwhelming to parents as it seems exciting to kids. Some parents, particularly those who work away from home, panic at the idea of having to plan three months of activities for their children; others resist planning because they want these months to be relaxed and unhurried. Often the child shatters this romantic ideal of a spontaneous, fun-filled time by walking into the living room or calling at work ten days into the summer and announcing, "There's nothing to do." Summer needs to be broken up by more than the daily arrival of the ice cream truck; children need, and usually appreciate, routine and structure. Kids have much more fun, and learn more, when there's plenty to do.

If you're like most people, you're very busy but also eager to help your child have a wonderful summer. This book is intended to give you lots of ideas for planning your child's summer and to help you benefit from the experiences of other parents. The activities will help your child play, relax, learn, grow, explore, and master new skills and return to school in the fall brimming with excitement and confidence.

Don't feel pressured to complete every chart included in these pages; decide which are easiest and quickest for you. I suggest many ways for you to combine a variety of structured activities with unstructured time to make this a fun summer for your child. Ultimately, I hope this book will inspire you and your child to come up with your own creative activities together. With planning, guidance, and encouragement, you can help your child have an interesting summer even without climbing Mount Everest or enrolling in flight school.

Chapter 1

· · · · · · · · · · · · · · · ·

Why Is Summer Important?

Each year, children ages six to twelve spend some 80 percent of their waking hours out of school. This unstructured time is equivalent to 4,680 hours, or 195 twenty-four-hour days. During this most important developmental stage in a child's life, summer accounts for nearly half of the unstructured time.

Some people consider school to be the center of a child's life and all other activities to be filler. But school was never intended to do it all. School is part of a process, and summer learning makes an enormous contribution to that process. Children don't turn off their eyes, ears, and minds when summer comes; they continue to learn. So does it matter in the long run how children use their summer hours? Yes!

Summertime is a valuable resource that must not be wasted. With plenty of opportunities for exciting activity, the months between school years are perfect for guiding children toward interests other than television and video games. Motivate your child to develop a keen interest or two, and expose her to a range of opportunities for developing "the other Rs"—resourcefulness and risk taking, responsibility, and relationships (see chapter 5)—while still providing ample time to play.

Children's out-of-school activities directly affect their performance in school. These activities will influence the rest of their childhood, adolescent, and adult lives. Although even the most active and motivated child wants and needs time to watch TV, talk on the phone, or just relax, children who benefit most from summer are those who spend much of their time actively doing things.

Children differ greatly in health, education, living circumstance, financial situation, social experience, and access to camp programs or community resources. All kids have one resource in common, though, and that is time. Across social classes, children are eight years old for exactly the same number of hours. What kids do with their time makes them different from other kids. What parents choose for their kids to do reflects family values, priorities, and aspirations. Most parents teach their children not to waste money but to spend it on things that matter. Similarly, children whose parents help them spend summertime inventively, enjoyably, and wisely have a great advantage.

A TIME TO GROW

Human development theory offers insights that help parents make intelligent decisions about their children's summer. Children between the ages of six and twelve—the period known as middle childhood—have tremendously different energy levels, attention spans, personalities, and interests. Some themes, however, remain constant. Children of these ages are active learners, explorers, discoverers, inventors, experimenters, and doers. With passionate intensity, these kids try to take in new information about the world, to grasp the rules of society, and to make sense of other people's behavior and of their relationship to time and distance and to the world.

Some recent theories may have implications for what children learn outside of school. One theory proposes that humans develop intelligence in seven relatively autonomous areas: logical-mathematical (science, math), linguistic (poetry, journalism), musical (composition, instrument playing), spatial (navigation, sculpting), bodily-kinesthetic (dancing, athletics), interpersonal (therapy, sales), and intrapersonal (self-knowledge). Some of these intelligences are obvious in a child's schoolwork, but others emerge in out-of-school activities. Summer is the perfect time to cultivate kinds of intelligence not expressed in the classroom and to expand on those brought out during the school year.

Nine-year-old Michelle was given an inexpensive camera and quickly mastered the basics of exposure, distance, film types, and lighting effects. She and her grandfather began taking "picture walks" together. Through this experience, Michelle developed visual sensitivity at an early age.

Confidence Building

Children ages six to twelve gain self-confidence when they progress rapidly in a particular area. Children can use the uninterrupted block of time during the summer to work on one or two activities or interests. They can improve at games, practice an instrument regularly, or go to a summer camp that fosters one particular interest. A child who sets aside a part of each day for a single activity can gain a sense of pride and accomplishment in that area.

One day when Eileen was ten, her mother saw an ad in the newspaper announcing free tennis lessons. Eileen enrolled and spent every day that summer playing tennis. Those free lessons helped her develop concentration, good sportsmanship, discipline, physical endurance, and lifelong friendships.

Social Development

In Groups

Children in middle childhood develop intense friendships with other children. Some experts, in fact, call this the gang period because of the strong ties children have with their peers. They often want to visit each other's houses, see each other's rooms and outdoor spaces, play with one another's things, play games with each other, spend the night together, and go places together.

When your child is with other children, he can sort out what the world is like and how he fits into it. He may realize when he is being too wild, too pompous, too silly, or too shy and change his behavior so he will get along better with others. Children in groups gradually gauge and adjust their ways of talking and acting in order to make and keep friends. Summer friendships usually involve cooperating or collaborating on activities, which encourages children to invest time in new projects or to try new sports.

Children develop social skills over the summer as they make new friends under the relaxed conditions of one long recess at the playground or camp. Children who attend overnight camps learn to compromise and share with others and develop independence and a sense of self. Bunkmates from early camping experiences may become lifelong friends. Often young people who have attended camp during middle childhood return as junior and senior counselors, ultimately gaining fulfilling leadership experiences.

Deciding whether or not to send your child to summer camp is difficult. All children experience some degree of homesickness, a healthy reaction to being away from home. Encouraging your child to stick with it and make new friends can only help her in the long run, and by the end of the session, she may not want to come home.

Dale first went to summer camp when he was seven years old. He lived in a big city and loved to play outdoors during the summer. At camp, he tried swimming, boating, water-skiing, tennis, softball, baseball, soccer, archery, arts and crafts, and drama. He made strong friendships and insisted on going back every year.

At age fifteen, Dale became a counselor-in-training; after that, he was a counselor for three years. When Dale was twenty-one, he was an assistant head counselor and organized the camp Olympics. These experiences taught him to compromise and share, to help others, and to be a team player.

Dale's camp experience even helped prepare him for college. Unlike many freshmen, he had already lived away from home and shared space with others. Now a lawyer, Dale still enjoys the friends he made at summer camp.

If you are reluctant to send your child away for a long period of time, look for a camp that offers one- or two-week sessions. Or, if your child doesn't seem ready for camp at all, schedule time for him to be with a group of children in a less structured setting. Swimming pools, playgrounds, and basketball courts are some possibilities.

With Best Friends

In a world of many friends, children in middle childhood often develop intense friendships with one or two other children, usually of the same sex. Between the ages of eight-and-a-half and ten, a child often finds her first "best friend." As the friendship develops, the child becomes sensitive to others and starts to think about ways to make her special friend happy.

Three times a week, Heather and her friend Amy, both eleven, worked with a sitter to design birthday cards, make bookmarks, create colorful small bags, and more. They went to shops to look for design ideas, sometimes following a theme that the sitter would suggest. One week, for example, they looked for sailboats on cards, paper, boxes, and T-shirts and then returned home to work on their own sailboat-related projects. Heather developed a sense of pride and felt her artwork was as good as some she had seen on the waterfront downtown.

Consider having your child and his best friend spend part of their summer together. Enroll them in the same activities part of the time, or have one child visit the other's family for a few days. It might seem like inviting more work, with two children to ask, "What is there to do?" but you will probably hear far less of that with two around than with one: the friends will find endless ways to entertain each other. Together, they might also have the courage to try an activity such as overnight camp that would be scary to one of them alone.

If your child will be apart from her best friend for much of the summer, suggest that she set aside time each week to write to her friend. This will help her develop her writing skills, document her activities, and reflect on the summer as it progresses.

With Adults and Older Kids

Part of a child's social development involves interactions with adults and older kids, both inside and outside the family. Summer is a great time for your children to pursue special interests with an influential older person such as a sitter, friend, grandparent, or other relative. An older friend can often keep a child interested and excited about things the two do together.

Damiano was ten years younger than his brother Paulo and keenly interested in journalism. One summer, Paulo, who was editor of his college newspaper, taught Damiano writing and editing skills. Every week, Damiano assisted Paulo on journalism assignments; during an eight-week period, Damiano wrote several short stories.

Cognitive Development

Curiosity and excitement about learning fuel children ages six to twelve. These kids think in ways that are reasonable and logical, especially regarding things that they know. Furthermore, kids in their middle childhood are able to integrate what they know. They enjoy playing Mancala, board games such as Monopoly or Hail to the Chief, and educational computer games that challenge them to understand and remember complicated rules. Reading opens new worlds to children, who absorb astonishing amounts of factual information. These kids talk constantly, describing scenes and people, telling interminable stories, recounting detailed information, and playing with expanding vocabularies. They are fascinated by classifications and often memorize vast systems of information—kinds of dinosaurs, names of Greek gods, and species of birds. They also sort smaller bits of knowledge into categories. This kind of classification leads naturally to collecting. Your child can collect and classify any of hundreds of types of things: rocks, minerals, coins, stamps, baseball cards, or sea life. Yard sales and flea markets can be treasure troves of collectibles. Visit these places, explore, and search with your child.

Middle childhood is a period of enormous curiosity about the natural world. Your child might be interested in insects, birds, weather, or geography. Help him pursue these interests through summer activities, such as building a weather station in the backyard, complete with barometer, thermometer, and weather vane; through reading; or through educational software, such as Where in the World Is Carmen Sandiego?

Daniel, an eight-year-old, looked out a window with binoculars and came up with a steady stream of observations, thoughts, and questions: "There's a katydid down there. Did you know that hummingbirds can't walk? Hey! I've got a nice, big, plump robin."

Even after he put down his binoculars, Daniel's thoughts continued. "I wonder if it's raining in China. We could call the weather in China. . . . I wish the scarlet tanagers would come back. They're so neat. . . . Mom, where's Arizona? Where's Wyoming?—wild and woolly and wacky Wyoming!"

Summer is also a great time to enroll your intellectually curious child in a reading program at a local library. Some communities offer summer writing projects for budding creative writers. Camps specialize in writing; computers; visual arts; music, drama, and dance; and scientific discovery.

Summer can include time for a child to bolster academic skills. If your child has had difficulties in school in the preceding year, set aside time each day to work on problem areas. Look for card games, board games, or educational software to address the academic skills that need work.

Development of Mastery

Children in middle childhood want to make things and master what they do. Human development theorist Erik H. Erikson explains that children ages six to ten develop healthy personalities based on a "sense of industry." This theorist refers to the enormous interest children this age have in learning how things work and in constructing practical things: tree houses, puppets, model castles. Failure to acquire these kinds of skills can lead to feelings of inferiority.

With this in mind, have your child create and build complicated structures at home: a fort, a raft, a soapbox racer, a model airplane. Children can work on these projects throughout the summer, enhancing them as they get new ideas. Based on these projects, discuss aspects of the physical world, such as buildings, bridges, and motors.

Physical Development

Children in this age group develop a growing sense of independence and self-esteem through physical activi-ties. As their motor skills develop, school-age children enjoy playing vigorously at four square, tennis, basketball, gymnastics, and other sports.

Some community programs conduct athletic camps a few nights or days each week. Summer camps may introduce children to a variety of sports or may focus on one particular sport. In any event, children learn to become team players and further their athletic skills.

Emotional Development

Children in middle childhood seem rather resilient emotionally. They may become sad, upset, or angry, but they usually get over these feelings quickly, apparently able to console themselves and their friends.

During the summer, school-age children are likely to be disappointed over such things as a canceled trip or outing. Not every activity you plan will be a success. When this happens, brainstorm for new ideas, plan something else, and go on.

Development of Independence

Children of just about any age want to be more independent. No matter what your child can do—tie her shoelaces, ride a bike, build a model, make a peanut butter sandwich—the key words are "by myself." Parents can help older children of this age group become more independent by, for example, allowing them to travel to visit friends or relatives over the summer. If your child is going to travel by public transportation, arrange beforehand for someone to be waiting when the child arrives at the other end; choose someone you can trust and your child can identify. Wait at the station until the bus or train has left, and instruct the child to call you upon arrival at the other end.

Brenda, age ten, was excited about a trip she took to visit her friend Sophia at the beach. "We stayed up all night and talked," Brenda later told her father. "We slept outside in a tent, and we went to this neat penny candy store. There were lots of minnows at the beach, and we made a huge castle. They said they wanted me to come back. I want to go back."

Paradoxically, structure makes children's independence possible. By providing structure in each day and in the physical environment, you can help children do things on their own. Be clear about expectations. Set realistic summer goals for your children, and help them organize their time so that they can reach these goals. Be patient, and reward each new development in independence.

You can be proud of your children when they accomplish things by themselves. Extreme independence is not the goal for school-age children, however. Children of this age cannot be completely responsible for their free time. Do not ask your kids to be alone all day; they will not thrive if forced to be independent.

PLAY: A PART OF EVERY DAY

As you begin to think about your child's summer, be careful not to overprogram. Remember that children this age need lots of time to play and to daydream. Play and playthings encourage mastery. When children play, they are in control. Children constantly learn and test their skills as they roller-blade, play kickball, shoot baskets, and make things out of paper, glue, wood, and fabric. A city block on a hot summer afternoon is rife with examples of children's ingenuity and creativity. Two children sit on a stoop playing a card game, while two others weave potholders. On the sidewalk, four girls jump rope and chant songs. On the corner, three boys squirt each other with a hose. All of these children are having fun, seizing the moment, learning how to be friends, collaborating, cooperating, exercising, understanding what makes a good sport, and experiencing their neighborhood.

No child will be happy if every moment of his or her summer is programmed with structured activity. All children need time to daydream, dress up, get into mischief, talk to themselves, play in a brook, and generally mess around. These activities are at the heart of childhood. Even when children tell jokes and throw water balloons, they can be making good use of their time. The best summer for any child, then, will include a careful balance of structured activity and unstructured time to play.

Chapter 2

· · · · · · · · · · · · · · · · ·

Gearing Up for Summer

Building a successful summer is more like digging a tunnel than like riding a bicycle. Don't expect to take an easy ride from June to September with your child in the backseat; rather, planning should be a collaborative effort that will deepen your knowledge of your child and your child's knowledge of the world. You won't simply be following colored lines on a map; you will be taking a trip that involves some guesswork, some good luck, and a lot of love.

Trust your intuitions, and try new ways of doing things. Help your child take a leap. You leap, too. Don't wait to figure out the "perfect" way to do things and end up waiting out your child's summer. To help children use their time meaningfully is to invest in the future. Enthusiasm will pay off. Together you can make this time so rich that it will help build your child's adult personality and lifelong interests.

PLAN EARLY

It is never too soon to start thinking about your child's summer—and if you're thinking about it, your child should be, too. Write down ideas during the winter. Talk to your child's teacher about interests that emerge during the school year and that you can help your child pursue through summer activities. Find out if you can help your child develop skills and confidence in problem areas through summer activities.

With the last month of school often given over to preparing for summer, and the first month to review, your child may be eager for extra challenges even before summer officially starts, and you may want to continue summer activities into the fall. Be aware, though, that your kid will need a break the week after school lets out. This time is often especially difficult for parents, because school programs have just ended and summer ones haven't started yet. The week before school starts is also difficult. You may want to schedule play dates with friends during these weeks, or organize cooperative activities that are fun and relaxing.

Involve Children

School-age children do best at activities they have helped to plan. Let children decide with you what the family will do and then look forward to doing those things. Planning a summer for your children with their involvement takes only a little more time than making choices without them and often keeps everyone happier. If a child resists an activity, try to distinguish real negative feelings from normal apprehension about new things. As one parent said about his children's reluctance to attend weekly ballet classes, "They don't want to go. But they want to be made to go."

In guiding your children, develop an authoritative style that is neither too lenient nor too strict. Establish clear limits, articulate your wishes, and don't give in to unreasonable demands. Negotiate conflicts by exchanging ideas until you come to a mutually agreeable solution. Try to have a sense of what's available and affordable in advance so that you can avoid setting up unrealistic expectations. If a child has his or her heart set on an activity that would be too expensive, see if a compromise is possible: if soccer camp is out of the question, look for a local club that offers free soccer coaching; if riding camp isn't possible, consider a few lessons over the course of the summer.

Expect Disappointments

Don't worry if your children don't react as positively to all experiences as you had thought they would. It's more important to provide a mix of activities—opportunities for children to grow in different ways—than to have each experience be perfect. Many families divide their summers among different places: home, the community, camp, and excursion or vacation destinations. Taking trips, having adventures, meeting people, learning new subjects, collecting mementos and knick-knacks, trying new foods, sleeping in new beds, hearing new noises, gaining new skills, and going to camp to explore new interests can all be enjoyable.

Maintain Flexibility

Flexibility is an essential element of every good summer. Mix equal parts of free time and organized activities. While structured activities allow children to play, learn, experiment, and explore with others, open spans of time allow them to do their own thing and relax. In addition, most parents are extremely busy; trying to do too much can leave you and your family miserable.

Because summer activities and programs are essentially optional, you might feel that forcing your child to go somewhere, practice the piano, or play baseball in the park makes you pushy. On the other hand, children do need encouragement and support, and sometimes even a little push. You will probably know by intuition when you are trying to do too much.

Develop the Other Rs

The other Rs—resourcefulness and risk taking, responsibility, and relationships—are critical aspects of growing up. Help your children develop independence by tuning in to their interests, locating appropriate resources, establishing routines, encouraging chores, guiding television and video watching, and teaching summer safety. See chapter 5 for more on the other Rs.

Anticipate Difficult Times

Children often complain that they have nothing to do. Instead of running to the video store to rent a movie, talk to your kids about ways to spend time when there is no structured activity going on. Often the hours preceding dinner become a strain for everyone around the house, including children. Consider ways to wind down from afternoon activities ahead of time. Bedtime is also a challenge. Perhaps one of the best ways to meet this challenge is to plan a routine with your child that allows time to read or play a simple card game before the lights go out.

Establish Routines

In middle childhood, children develop problem-solving skills and a logical understanding of time, space, and distance. These children are particularly eager to make sense of time and will pester you with questions like "How long till bedtime?" "How soon does school start?" "When will we get there?" Summer routines will help your child understand how time works.

Most families establish routines to help members get things done and provide a sense of security. These routines are often so natural that outsiders will not even see them. In general, families that do not actually establish and talk about their organization of time fall into conflict. You can best help your children understand your family's routines by talking to them frequently about how they fit into the plans. Talking itself, in fact, should be part of the plans. Make breakfast or dinner regular sharing times for the family, or agree upon another time to meet.

If you already have established routines, you will probably change some parts of them during the summer. Make sure your children understand the new routine. Ask each child to repeat his or her plans for the day. "Who is meeting you today?" "Which bus are you taking today?" Discuss ways in which the routine might break down when you aren't around. Think through solutions together.

Organize Your Home

Physical spaces influence a child's behavior. In a disorganized household, children must depend on adults for information. If your kids know where things are, and if the things they need are within reach, they can get what they want, use it, and put it away by themselves.

You may want to get ready for summer by reorganizing parts of your home where children will spend the most time. Helping with this activity will give kids a sense of control over their environment and a feeling of anticipation toward summer fun.

Communicate Your Values

Think about what's important to you and share your ideas with your children. Don't feel pressured to do something just because another family is doing it. If something doesn't make sense to you, think about why it doesn't, and discuss it as early as possible with your child.

Create a Calendar

To help your children plan out summer, start with a weekly calendar, build it into a monthly one, and, finally, put together a plan that might work for the entire summer. Planning ahead gives children a sense of control and helps them learn to use time effectively. In June, they can look forward to summer activities with excitement; in September, they can look back with a sense of accomplishment.

Calendars help the family to understand each person's daily routines, the rhythms of the week, and

Summer Home Preparation

- With your child, create a Family Message Center (see appendix). Start by posting a working summer calendar in a place where everyone can read it; have children help you mark entries on it. Around the calendar or on a bulletin board, post lists of fun things to do, neat places to go, great books and magazines to read, favorite TV shows to watch and videos to consider renting, healthful snacks to make, summer safety rules, summer responsibilities and chores, and phone numbers to call. The phone list should include numbers for fire, police, and medical help. Never leave notes on the front door.

- Choose one accessible cabinet for storing children's art and game supplies. Include drawing supplies, paints, rubber stamps, construction paper, scissors, markers, and glue.

- Choose another accessible cabinet for plastic eating utensils, paper plates, and snack foods.

- Set aside a time at the end of the day for children to gather toys, art supplies, and so on and put them away. This will increase their sense of responsibility and ownership.

the patterns that shape a month. Children who can see a routine written down feel secure, knowing they can check it again. Remember that you don't have to fill every block of time; children need unstructured time to play or wind down. Calendars help children value that free time, because the kids learn to see time as part of an overall pattern. As children add vacation schedules, trips, parties, weeks at camp, daily activities, and other events to the calendar, they begin to realize what portion of their time is organized, and how. They know when they will go to camp, hiking for the weekend, or with a friend to the lake; when they will have free time; and when they can make decisions about the use of specific periods of time.

Using an oversized monthly calendar makes keeping track of time both visual and accessible. You can make a separate calendar for each child or a family calendar for everyone's activities. On heavy paper, mark a grid for each week and then one for each month. You and your children can then begin to fill in activities on specific days. Be sure to include birthdays and other family celebrations. You might also include interesting facts from *The Guinness World Book of Records,* unusual historical anniversaries from *Chase's Annual Events,* or quotes from famous people such as Dr. Seuss or John Ciardi.

The calendar can be a lively record of tentative and firm arrangements, frequently corrected or confirmed.

Children will learn most from the experience if they design and make calendars on their own. They can include facts and pictures about what they plan to do, using paper, colored markers, stencils, rubber stamps, heart- and other-shaped punches, ziggy scissors, pictures cut from magazines, and so on. As summer progresses, children can add photographs, covers from books or board games, and three-dimensional objects such as shells, sand, and dried flowers.

Referring to the calendar each day will give children an awareness of their activities, responsibilities, and even moods. Give children "mood stickers" to mark especially fun days or not-so-good days. Have children add details of experiences after they occur. If you write down things your children observed or learned each day, children can look back on these experiences at the end of the summer.

Many families put calendars where everyone can read them, so the family can see at a glance what is going on. With a calendar, you and your family can tell where scheduling will be tight, anticipate exciting times, and prepare for periods of boredom or rushing around. Each evening, you can review the next day's activities with your children, and you can remind them again in the morning of what that day will hold.

Also try making a week-at-a-glance plan. Sitters can use this kind of calendar to plan fun activities. Some families put the working calendar in the middle of a bulletin board and replace it weekly or monthly. Permanent information posted around the calendar might include emergency phone numbers, ideas for reading, recipes for snacks, fun things to do when there is nothing to do, summer responsibilities, creative artwork, summer safety rules, and so on.

TUNE IN TO YOUR CHILD

Some parents feel they know their children very well, and indeed they do. But it is always good to take a fresh look at your children and to try to understand them even better.

Don't try to plan a whole summer in one night. Think about a few issues at a time. Figuring out exactly what your children want to do may feel like following a trail of breadcrumbs through a forest. Particularly with young kids, who often say they want to do everything,

it's easy to follow a false trail and end up lost. If, however, you trust your intuition, think about what you most enjoyed about your childhood, listen carefully to what your children say, and watch them at work, you will find that planning is rewarding and rather easy. Focus on your children and discuss options with them. Your input is important; the input of your children is doubly so.

Eight-year-old Elaine loves animals and is always talking about pandas, dolphins, seals, elephants, lions, tigers, and bears. She knows all about endangered species and is interested in dinosaurs. During the summer she could

- go to the library and get books about one favorite animal each week. She could read about what each animal eats, where and how it lives, and how it seems to feel about humans.

- subscribe to magazines such as *National Geographic WORLD*.

- visit nearby zoos, aquariums, animal farms, and natural history museums.

- collect posters and pictures of favorite animals.

- visit a local animal shelter and play with the animals waiting for adoption.

- make animal cookies and animal puppets.

- collect stuffed animals and make elaborate homes for them.

- write to preservation groups such as the World Wildlife Fund.

- watch television programs such as *Wild Kingdom* or *Jacques Cousteau* or subscribe to the Discovery Channel.

- look for software that would give her a role as an explorer in an environment such as the ocean or a tropical rainforest.

The following steps can help you tune in to your child's interests and plan a fun summer. This process will help you choose community resources, camps, or other programs and plan excursions or a vacation. Once you consider your child's interests, you will know what sports equipment, art supplies, or games and backyard activities will be most fun and worthwhile for your child and your family.

Trust Your Intuitions

Much of what you do as a parent is intuitive, based on love for your children and a desire for them to have a rich, enjoyable, and productive childhood. Thanks to years of experience, you know best how to interpret your child's behavior, and recognize signs of happiness, excitement, eagerness, frustration, fatigue, overstimulation, loneliness, and boredom. You know your child's strengths, temperament, and needs. Your instincts about what will interest your child are sound; use them.

The following questions will give you new insights into your child. Remember: you know your child best.

1. How would you describe your child's temperament? What are his or her strengths? Weaknesses? Likes? Dislikes?

2. Have your child's interests changed over time? How? Why?

3. Did your child seem to have enough to do last summer? What did you learn from last summer?

4. What were the high points of your child's summer last year? What were the low points? Why?

5. Did anything happen last summer that was painful or negative for your child? What did you or your child learn from it?

6. In what area does your child seem to need the most help? Can you do anything about it this summer?

7. Has your child become involved with something because of a friend? Is it turning out to be a good experience for your child? Could this be a starting point for an activity this summer?

You may find it helpful to think about your own summer experiences, both positive and negative. Most parents consciously and unconsciously try to structure their children's middle childhood to give them what they most appreciated when they were kids and to avoid what they didn't like. Remembering your childhood summers will help you understand your child's perspective.

The following questions will help you remember summers during middle childhood. Share your recollections with your children.

1. What did you like to do best during the summer? What are your fondest memories of your summers?

2. Did you enjoy certain activities during the summer that you still enjoy today? What are they?

3. Who got you started in those activities? When? If you hadn't gotten started in them at that age, do you think you would be pursuing them today?

4. Did you have a favorite place to go? Where was it? How did you get there? What did you do there?

5. What important lessons did you learn from your parents or other adults during your summers?

Watch and Observe

Often you can learn a lot about your children's interests by watching what they do in their spare time. What games do they play? What outdoor toy or piece of equipment is always out of the closet? Where do your children like to go? Certain materials, equipment, and experiences have meaning for each child. By carefully watching your child at play and at work, you can come up with even more ideas for summer.

Brian loves baseball cards. He can quote facts and figures about many of the players and is interested in talking or playing baseball with anyone who knows the game. Over the summer, Brian and his sisters could

- visit the Baseball Hall of Fame in Cooperstown, New York.

- go to baseball games and learn how to score the game on the official scorecard.

- go to baseball card shows and talk to collectors.

- write to players' fan clubs.

- ask local coaches how statistics are taken.

- join a Little League team.

- get some books about baseball and the lives of baseball players.

- design a baseball board game.

- set up a baseball-card-trading club with friends.

- buy or construct a pitching net and practice throwing strikes.

Think about the sorts of things that interest your children. Do they like to use poster paints or clay? Do they love backpacking, playing baseball, or bicycling? Are they crazy about computers, drama, fishing, horseback riding, mountain climbing, music, sailing, tennis, or swimming? What sorts of games do your children play? Are they curious about cameras, telescopes, or microscopes? Do they enjoy browsing in particular types of stores? What kinds of movies or television programs do they like? Do they enjoy going to a particular museum or sporting event? When your children pretend, who or what do they pretend to be? Do they have any special needs that should be considered?

Over the next few days, observe your children and list the specific materials, equipment, experiences, or tools that interest them. These unspoken affinities explain a great deal about a child's likes. Jot down notes and put them in a folder for summer planning.

Listen and Learn

Listen and learn from your children. Ask each child the following questions and use the answers to help you determine areas that most interest your child and to search for resources. What's fun? What's fabulous for summer? Listen to what your child says. Resist feeling overwhelmed, depressed, or discouraged by your child's candor. Remember, children vary in ability and age, and this makes a difference in the way they answer questions. Try to understand the way your children think and what they want to do. Take notes; no one can rely completely on memory. When looking over your notes, ask yourself: What is my child telling me? What is my child most curious about now? What might my child want me to know more about?

Ask these questions when you and your child are both relaxed. Let your child talk freely; try not to answer the questions for him or her. Don't ask all the questions at once: ask two or three at one time and another two or three a few days later.

1. If you could do anything this summer, what would you do? Describe it.

2. What is your favorite thing to do in the summer?

3. Would you like to go to camp? A day camp or an overnight camp? Why?

4. Would you like to do things around the community? What? Why?

5. Would you like to go someplace this summer? Where? Why?

6. What do your friends do in the summer? Do you wish you could do these things, too?

7. What do you like to do at the playground? What don't you like?

8. Would you prefer doing something with a friend, or by yourself?

9. What are you good at? What do you think you are not so good at?

10. What do you wish you were better at?

11. What do you wish you could do that you don't know how to do?

12. What do you like to do with the family? Where would you like to go with the family?

13. What did you do last summer that you want to do again this summer? What don't you want to do again?

14. What is your best time of day in the summer? Why?

15. What is your worst time of day in the summer? Why?

Over a period of time, ask your children to draw pictures or create collages showing the things they would like to do this summer. Watch what your children draw and create from pictures in magazines and catalogs. As your child cuts out these pictures, have him or her put together those of greatest interest. One child might put together seascapes and swim gear, another hundreds of animals, and yet another a collection of cars. Children like to cut out and glue together their favorite things to do.

The Yes, No, Maybe Chart (see appendix) is a list of things that children this age do. Filling out this chart gives kids new ideas and shows parents what the kids are really interested in doing. Kids like putting stick-on dots beside the activities they would really like to try. (You will need to help children who don't read well.) Many kids, especially young ones, want to do absolutely everything and will check boxes until they run out of chart, which is fun but defeats the purpose. To prevent this, work on the chart with your child over a period of time. If necessary, tell your child to choose only one or two activities for the summer.

If the chart is too extensive, make your own list, including only resources that you know are available in your community and affordable for your family. You'll want to look at the Yes answers first, but the Maybe answers can reveal most in some cases. A child who checks Maybe for go on nature walks, look at stars, learn more about whales and endangered animals, make things with shells, and collect rocks and fossils might find nature studies a perfect match.

Make Decisions

Turn summer interests into actions. A perfect plan for your child's summer won't just happen: parents and children need to make decisions. As you sift through your notes and charts, ideas will emerge as strong possibilities for summer activities and plans.

When it comes time to make the final decisions, don't lose sight of your family's values or style of child-rearing. Time and money may be concerns; consider what any plan will require of you before making a commitment.

If you're nervous about making decisions for your child, take heart: many adults look back on their decisive parents with gratitude. Children are often timid about experimenting and want parents to encourage them to try new activities and follow through.

When asked how she fostered her children's interests, Priscilla, a mother of five, said, "I waited until an interest bubbled up; then I pounced on it. I tried to demonstrate my sensitivity by waiting for each child to give a lead, and then I showed my love by following through on those interests."

Supporting your child's interests doesn't mean moving in with a world-famous gymnastic instructor. You can find an organization, club, program, or youth group for nearly every interest imaginable. If your child wants to try woodworking, calligraphy, or chess, look for a group of like-minded people in your area. See chapter 3 for activities that will help turn interests into actions.

Build upon Interests

As your children's summer interests emerge, design activities based on those interests that will stimulate your children in important developmental areas. Activities don't have to be elaborate or expensive. If your child is interested in birds, for example, help her use binoculars to study birds, build a bird feeder for the backyard or window, sign her up for an organized bird-watching class, check out library books about birds, or go to a pet store that carries a variety of birds. Involve the rest of the family by going on nature walks. Look into day or overnight camps that offer hiking, mountain climbing, or environmental studies.

Several days before a beach trip, take your children to the library to get books on the ocean, marine life, and arts and crafts using shells. While at the beach, explore what you've learned. Using pails, shovels, cups, and molds, children can build a sand castle. Take along plastic people to live in the castle. Collect beach objects such as shells, sticks, feathers, and rocks to create unique designs in the sand. Before you leave, collect souvenirs from the sea. When you get home, have your children use shells to make mobiles, jewelry, or ornaments. A child might decide to write or tape a story called "My Day at the Beach."

When Ian was seven, he and his family took a vacation in the Florida Keys. Ian was introduced to saltwater fishing and loved it. He quickly mastered the intricacies of fishing rods and reels and of baiting hooks and removing fish from the line. He got up early in the morning and hung around the docks, watching the commercial fishers go out and peering into the water to see the fish swimming beside the pilings. By the end of the week in Florida, Ian had learned the name of every fish caught there and had convinced his family to take a tour of a coral reef on a glass-bottomed boat. He also bought himself a National Parks Service book on fish.

After his family came home, Ian checked out books on fish and fishing from his school and neighborhood libraries. He found out about a group called Urban Anglers that held daylong demonstrations at the local river. One August afternoon, he looked in the Yellow Pages under F, discovered an ad for fishing with the Quincy Bay Flounder Fleet, dialed the number, and learned how to fish with the group. When bluefish were running, he talked his father into taking him, and they spent an entire day in a chartered fishing vessel. Ian's biggest catch, thirty-two inches long, was the largest fish caught on the boat that day.

By now, Ian's knowledge of fish and fishing was far greater than his parents', and he needed contact with other knowledgeable adults to satisfy his curiosity. He persuaded the proprietor of a bait shop to take him on several excursions and went often to the New England Aquarium and the Peabody Museum's exhibit on fish.

Use the following questions to help you build upon your child's interests.

1. What kind of information does the library, museum, or any special group have on your child's interest?

2. Are there games to go to or amateur leagues to join?

3. What performances, demonstrations, and lectures could you and your child go to?

4. Could the whole family participate in some related activities?

5. Could your child write to companies, groups, or clubs for information or freebies?

6. What could your child make, create, and build around the interest?

7. What sort of creative things could expand the interest? Puzzles? Board games? Writing projects?

8. Are any contests related to the interest? Any books?

9. Do any children or adults nearby have the same interests? Are there groups to join?

When looking for ways to expand on interests, don't overwhelm your child with your enthusiasm. Your questions and advice should point to new directions. Some children need only a small bit of adult help and will do most of the pursuing on their own. The more investigating the child does, the prouder he or she will feel of the result.

Chapter 3

Discovering Summer Possibilities

Once you and your children have a sense of what they want to do this summer, your next task is to decide how they're going to do it. Parks and recreation programs, camp counselors, relatives, sitters, coaches, trips, and friends can all contribute to a summer of exploration.

All aspects of child-rearing lead parents into new territory, but middle childhood is an especially exciting period. Your child's curiosity and newfound interests will have you experiencing your community and other places as if for the first time—entering buildings you've walked by for years, visiting camps you've only heard about, reading parts of the newspaper you've always skipped, making new friends and connections. These experiences expand a child's knowledge and appreciation of others, and parents often have as much fun as their kids do.

You may want to start out by pursuing programs related to interests your child has already expressed. If you broaden your search, however, you may find a terrific summer program and, after discussing it with your child, discover that it's something she or he hadn't thought about before but would love to do.

Following are some ideas for learning about summer options.

- Look up all the resources in your community that might be summer oriented. Talk with teachers, principals, counselors, or members of youth-serving organizations.

- Ask your children what they especially enjoyed last summer. If one describes the great time she had examining a friend's coin collection, have a friend who travels bring back foreign currency. If another enjoyed watching a hockey game, look into hockey programs in the area.

- Talk with other children about what they did last summer. Ask what was good and what was bad.

- Talk with other parents about resources they have found helpful.

- Learn about children's programs sponsored by local museums, zoos, schools, sporting clubs and facilities, nature groups, churches and religious groups, or national or state parks. Ask about days or hours you can get in free.

- Find out if your local pool or lake offers a swimming program or has designated children's swimming hours (with or without a lifeguard) and whether children must be accompanied by an adult.

- Learn what summer children's programs and activities your local parks and recreation department offers. Inquire about special groups or organized trips.

- Find out if youth organizations such as 4-H, the Ys, Scouts, Boys and Girls Clubs, Camp Fire, or

Big Brothers and Big Sisters offer summer programs in your community.

❖ Contact vocational and high schools about summer courses in computers, carpentry, and so on.

❖ Check out local theater groups. Some offer beginners hands-on learning experiences in performance and stagecraft.

❖ Make a list of area colleges and universities. Many offer summer programs in physical education, drama, music, dance, archaeology, and so on.

❖ Ask if your local parent-teacher association (PTA) keeps a file of parents' and children's evaluations of summer programs previously conducted in your community.

❖ Compile a list of possible summer camps, using recommendations from your local library, PTA, school, municipal parks, churches, and other parents. Consider day camps and overnight camps; general camps that combine arts and crafts, sports, swimming, and drama; and specialized camps—such as hockey, tennis, computer, music, or language—that focus on one activity but also include general camp experiences. Camps vary greatly in price, quality, duration, capacity, and travel distance. The American Camping Association (ACA) and other organizations sponsor camp fairs in various parts of the country. Use reference books on camps and camping (see the resources section in this book).

❖ Pay attention to local media. Television and radio stations regularly broadcast community events calendars and information about family-oriented activities. Many newspapers publish information on summer camp opportunities as early as February or March.

❖ Some consultants and referral services provide information and contacts with camp directors. Ask plenty of questions while using such services and again before enrolling your child in a camp. If the answers you receive are not satisfactory, check with your local Better Business Bureau or Chamber of Commerce.

❖ Many cities have parents' newsletters and magazines giving information on kid-oriented tours and events. Newspaper classifieds and the Yellow Pages may prove helpful in finding them. Save these for future reference.

❖ Get your child a library card. Libraries offer free summer reading groups, film series, and other educational activities for children. Ask your child's teacher for information about such programs. Also ask for a recommended reading list.

❖ Contact your local child-care resource and referral offices for information on specific programs for school-age children, such as day camps or organized sports.

❖ Ask your employer about services available for working parents.

After you have completed a list of resources, begin calling or writing for more information. Set aside a block of time to do this, if possible; otherwise, split up the job over several days, or get a friend or relative to help. (You may want to copy the Telephone Information Sheet included in this book.) Be persistent. As you continue networking, you'll be amazed at how many resources for children there are, even in small towns.

Call early to make reservations. Programs in your community might be booked early, especially if they're inexpensive. Camps—especially popular ones—have specific application deadlines.

As you gather summer information, narrow down your choices, keeping in mind your family's limits. Eliminate all camps or programs your family can't afford. Financial aid for many summer camps and programs is limited and not well advertised, so if you need aid, ask about it specifically. You may be able to cut costs for sports equipment by shopping at thrift stores or at sports equipment exchanges held by schools and organizations. Some stores specialize in used sporting goods. Look for music stores that rent instruments, and check the want ads for second-hand recreational equipment. Note that camps often provide all the equipment children need, so your child may need little more than clothes and a toothbrush.

Time, money, and transportation are key factors. Don't consider any activity that requires transportation you can't arrange or time you don't have. And before signing up for any program, make sure it is consistent with your family values.

If everyone has responded to your requests for information and you have notebooks full of interesting

TELEPHONE INFORMATION SHEET

Activity/Organization/Camp_____

Telephone Number _____

Contact Person _____

Brief Description _____

_____

Ages _____

Cost _____

How Long _____

Starting Date _____

General Impressions _____

Issues Important to Our Family _____

_____

possibilities, congratulations. But don't put your feet up yet. You still need to sort through what you've found and decide what your family's options are.

Divide summer resources outside the home into community programs, camps, sitters, coaches, and others. You and your child will probably choose a balance of these options, perhaps concentrating on one.

COMMUNITY PROGRAMS

Activities near the home—including those sponsored by community resources and parks and recreation programs—are often the easiest to find out about. You can probably get recommendations from friends or other parents about the best local instructors and programs. If your children are like most, they will be home for at least part of the summer, and community programs can offer a rich array of options.

Particularly with community programs, you may find surprises. When checking out a computer-programming course, for instance, you may discover a class in making Mexican pottery. When planning trips, you may find exciting things to see or do that you

hadn't expected. Take advantage of these unexpected opportunities. Above all, be flexible!

Katie always loved being outdoors. On her own, she learned about gardening and growing vegetables. She also enjoyed cooking and crafts. The summer she was nine years old, Katie attended 4-H camp to learn more about gardening and crafts. When she got there, she immediately fell in love with animals. She spent hours in the barnyard feeding the pigs and looking at the horses. Eventually, Katie became a veterinarian.

Unfortunately, some communities have limited resources, so you may have few options. Look carefully at each program, and check the reputation of the organization involved. Make sure that the activity you and your child choose is right for everyone involved.

Following are some questions you could ask about community resources.

1. How often does your program meet? What is the schedule?

2. Are missed sessions a problem? Are there make-up sessions?

3. Where is the program offered? Can one get there by public transit?

4. What is the fee? Do we pay by the week or by the month? Is there a scholarship program?

5. If we cancel, do we get a refund? How many sessions must we pay for initially? Must we buy or rent any equipment?

6. Who are the counselors? Who is the instructor?

7. How much experience has the instructor had? What do other people say about this person's skills? Could I get references?

8. How will progress be reported to parents?

9. What are the ages, sexes, and experience levels of the other children signed up? Are there likely to be other children my child will know?

10. Is it possible to contact other families to work out carpools?

11. How structured is the program? Is it part of a series? Is another level offered? If so, what requirements are involved?

12. Do you sponsor any free and/or special summer events?

CAMPS

Some kids have happy memories of camp and tell wonderful stories about the time they locked a friend out of the cabin or the picnic when the bear nearly ate all the sandwiches. Others go on and on about the horrible food, the kids they didn't like, the poison ivy, the time they threw up in their sleeping bag, and how they waited frantically for packages and letters. Be aware that some children are ready to go to camp earlier than others. The fact that Amadeus down the street is spending the summer at a music program in Germany doesn't mean that your Elizabeth is ready to be away from home for an extended period of time. Some children can handle day camps, but not overnight ones. Most children make it clear if they do not feel ready for overnight camp, but if you're not sure, think about whether your child is comfortable sleeping in other people's houses—with friends or relatives, for example. How far away from home has your child gone alone? Is she comfortable in new settings, or does it take her a long time to adjust? Does she like being independent?

Different camps appeal to different kids. General camps provide an array of activities and give campers a wider variety of outdoor experiences. Specialty camps, on the other hand, allow children to concentrate on a single activity, such as hockey, writing, or environmental issues. When choosing a camp, match your child's needs to the program. Don't send a child who hates competition to a camp that has constant meets and matches.

Camps are usually either private or agency sponsored. Individuals or groups own most private camps, though some are funded by endowments. Agency-sponsored camps include those run by such groups as the Ys, Scouts, Jewish community centers, and Catholic or Protestant churches. Social service agencies often run camps for children with special needs. An agency-sponsored camp has the advantage of a national reputa-tion, and many locations across the country may make it easier for you to get your child to and from camp.

Cristy wrote the following letter from space camp when she was ten:

Dear Gracie:

Thank you for the baseball cards. Happy Birthday. At Space Camp we got to experience weightlessness. We also got to go on a mission. A mission was where you could pick a position (I chose principal investigator) and you would be handed a script and you would go on a simulated mission. I was down at Mission Control. Our mission was to launch Space Shuttle Discovery. I had to repair a satellite. We also hung around Kennedy Space Center (where we got to see a whole bunch of movies) and visited U.S. Astronaut Hall of Fame.

Love, Cristy

To find information about specific camps, refer to the latest *Guide to Accredited Camps,* or write to the

ACA. Talking with other parents can also help you determine if a particular camp experience would suit your child's interests and sensibilities.

If possible, visit a camp you're considering while it is in session. Observe campers in various situations. In what sorts of activities are they involved? Do they seem enthusiastic? What role are counselors playing? How well do they interact with campers? Are campers involved in creative projects, such as building a birdhouse? Does there appear to be a sense of team spirit?

Be sure to inquire about accreditation, references, insurance, food service, and counselors' qualifications, and examine the camp's physical facilities to determine the quality of basic sanitation and maintenance.

Following are some questions you might ask a camp director.

1. How do campers get to the camp? Is there transportation from the bus station, airport, or nearby city to the camp? How much will transportation cost?

2. What is housing like? Are sleeping spaces well ventilated and comfortable? Do the kids have individual lockers? Are the bathrooms indoors? Do the cabins have electricity? Where do the counselors live?

3. How sanitary is the camp? What's the food like? Is the water safe?

4. How do parents keep track of their child's progress? What are the channels of communication, both routine and emergency?

5. What kind of medical arrangements are provided? Does a doctor or nurse live at the camp? What happens if an injury occurs away from camp, like on a camping trip? Is there a hospital nearby?

6. Who goes to the camp? What is the average age of campers? What religious and ethnic groups are represented?

7. What kind of leaders will your child have? What is the camper-to-counselor ratio? Are counselors screened? What references does the camp director have?

8. What is the camp's philosophy? What is its attitude about competitiveness?

9. Does the camp offer scholarships? Tuition refunds?

10. Can the camp give you some names of former campers as references?

11. What is the camp's policy on possessing or using drugs and alcohol?

SITTERS

If you need a sitter, look for one who is both reliable and energetic. Consider all of your needs. Do you want someone who can take your child to a swimming lesson or shopping for a birthday present? Take into account your child's age, maturity, and temperament when hiring a sitter.

Six- to twelve-year-olds can get along with a range of sitters. Don't limit your choices; consider both males and females, younger and older people, or people whose cultural or ethnic background your child might find interesting. Look for a sitter whose interests could intrigue your child or a group of children. Does the person know batik? Kite making? Sailing? A foreign language? Sitters with special talents might be willing to provide lessons in addition to child care. One family hired a sitter who taught cartoon drawing for two hours each week. In another family, a high school soccer player worked on soccer skills with the three children. You may want to consider hiring a sitter jointly with other parents and having the sitter care for the children all together or trade off hours among the families.

Following are suggestions for questions to ask when interviewing a sitter.

1. I/we need a sitter to care for _____ children, aged _____, for _____ hours each week. The pay is $___ per hour. Would you be interested?

2. What is your experience with children of this age?

3. Can you provide the names and phone numbers of two families for whom you have worked?

4. What kinds of activities do you like to do with kids?

5. What kinds of activities did you especially enjoy as a child?

6. What are your hobbies and interests? Are you willing to share some of them? What are some of the things you like best?

7. How have you spent your last two summers?

8. What are some of the ways in which you set limits and discipline children this age?

9. Do you smoke?

10. Do you have a driver's license? Can you help with transportation? Do you have your own car? What kind of insurance coverage do you have?

11. What are your career goals?

12. How would you handle an emergency? Are you trained in first aid? Cardiopulmonary resuscitation (CPR)?

COACHES

Coaches can have a strong influence on a child in middle childhood. Whether you are hiring a coach to work with your child alone or with a group, interview that person thoroughly. In community-sponsored sports, you have little if any choice about hiring coaches, but you can observe practices and attend games before arranging for your child to participate. How does the coach feel about girls participating in group sports? What are his or her attitudes about winning and losing? This is a critical question—the wrong attitude from a coach can discourage a child's participation in the sport. A coach's reaction to successes, frustrations, and setbacks—reflected in comments made to the players after an easy victory or a tough loss—should give you an idea of what to expect from this person. Make sure the coach is right for your child.

Following are suggested questions to use when interviewing a coach.

1. How were you trained and certified in your sport?

2. How many games are there in the season? How many practices?

3. Are you interested in working with a small group of children in our community? Do you have a block of time available? When?

4. What time of day and how long are games and practices?

5. What sort of child benefits most from being involved in this sport?

6. What expenses should we expect for travel, uniforms, equipment, and so on?

7. How do you encourage good sportsmanship? (Does the prospective coach strike you as a positive role model?)

8. Are your expectations different for boys and girls? If so, how?

9. How do you determine who will be on the starting team?

10. Who or what determines how long and how much each child will play in a game?

11. How important is it to you to have a winning team? How important do you feel it should be to the players?

12. What would you do to encourage the growth of a natural athlete or an uncoordinated child?

13. Do you provide nutritional counseling if it's important for participating in the sport?

14. Do you schedule regular water or snack breaks during games and practices?

15. How do you ensure safe playing conditions? Are there any hazards particular to this sport?

16. Will you check to make sure that players are wearing eye, head, face, mouth, and/or body protection at all times while on the playing field?

17. Are you trained in emergency procedures, first aid, CPR, and so on?

18. What insurance coverage does the team or organization have in case a child is injured? What liability, if any, do parents have in this type of situation?

INSTRUCTORS, ARTISTS, AND MUSICIANS

When considering an instructor, look first for expertise. Who teaches flute? What is the best place to learn macramé or photography? Next, look for people who are trained to work with children and who have an apparent love of teaching. If possible, arrange to observe a class or lesson, either alone or with your child or another parent. Be sure you understand completely all financial obligations, including fees, instrument rental if applicable, and specific equipment and supplies that you will be expected to provide.

In a personal interview, or through recommendations, do your best to assess a candidate's reliability, knowledge of the field, and rapport with children. Does the person appear enthusiastic? Flexible? Engaging enough to motivate children? Dependable about keeping appointments? Does he or she seem to develop a sense of camaraderie and respect among all involved? Ask artists how they would teach art to children this age. What sort of projects would they recommend? Do they feel the process or the product is more important?

Following are questions you might ask an instructor, an artist, or a musician.

1. What are the age, physical, and reading requirements for this particular training?

2. What do you see as your expertise in helping children this age to learn?

3. How much practice do you expect of children during the summer?

4. What expectations do you think we could realistically establish for children over the summer?

5. What are your ideas and methods for maintaining a child's interest in the subject or lessons?

6. Do you offer both individual and group instruction? How many children are likely to be in a group?

7. What sort of children benefit the most from this training?

8. How long have you been teaching? What are your background and qualifications?

9. Can you provide the names and phone numbers of two families for whom you have worked?

10. What teaching methods do you use? To what extent do you foster and encourage creative expression?

11. What other skills and abilities might a child develop by participating in this endeavor?

12. What is your summer schedule like? How often would you recommend lessons?

13. What suggestions do you have for parents to support their child's studies at home?

CREATIVE COOPERATIVES

An alternative to finding a summer program that meets your child's needs is joining together with other families and coming up with your own activities for children. In a cooperative, parents design the program themselves and can be creative and flexible about content and structure. The social setting is generally smaller, more personal, and less pressured than in organized groups. Organizing cooperative arrangements for a day, a week, or several weeks can be empowering. Parents and children alike develop friendships with the people involved.

Parents can make special cooperative arrangements to match a child's interest and skill level, to fit family schedules, or to meet the needs of a group of children. Making arrangements often involves organizing networks so that children can participate in creative activities such as dance, guitar lessons, or swimming; or arranging for an adult to teach calligraphy or cooking. Excursions to museums, wildlife sanctuaries, or archaeological sites also involve parental collaboration.

Groups of parents often hire instructors or coaches to teach gymnastics, swimming, flute lessons—or whatever their children have shown a common interest in pursuing. The right instructor will nurture that interest, help children develop their skills, and encourage them to excel.

Creative cooperatives help families solve time, money, and transportation problems and create a more flexible setting for a child. In one community, a group of college students who had spent their childhood summers together decided to offer a two-week camp for children ages five to nine. The college kids took turns planning activities for the half-day program; the group visited a local dairy farm and milked the cows, swam, and had a cookout and sing-along. The children wrote their own play and designed costumes and props. On the last night, they put on the play for the adults of the community.

If you plan a summer cooperative, be aware of potential problems. Most obviously, the entire setup can fall apart if families are not flexible. Working agreements are sometimes so vague that misunderstandings occur. Frequent phone calls, reminders, written instruction, and expressions of gratitude become essential. As you design a cooperative arrangement, ask potential members to discuss the following questions to make sure you agree about goals, structure, and time commitment. It may be useful to meet periodically to assess how well the cooperative is working.

1. How many hours a week will my child be involved?

2. How many hours a week will I be involved? Can someone else take over my shift if I cannot be there?

3. What rules of behavior can we agree on for all kids involved?

4. What food or other supplies do I have to provide?

5. What are our goals for the cooperative? Do we all agree on them?

6. Do any activities require parental consent or insurance?

7. What is our plan in case of medical or other emergency?

8. Are the trips that we planned realistic? Has any of us taken these trips before?

Following are examples of cooperatives that some families have organized.

Theme Week

Five families in one neighborhood planned a summer for their children, who ranged in age from about five to twelve. Each family was chief counselor for two weeks, and an adult helper was hired. The parent in charge shaped the week and shared his or her interests and skills with the children. Each week had a different theme:

❖ planting a garden and making a scarecrow

❖ creating, building, and inventing things

❖ making masks and putting on a show

❖ making ice cream and cooking

❖ exploring the city or going hiking

In addition, each day involved an element of surprise: lunch in the park, a picnic, bubbles, a trip to a museum, a walk to a great ice cream shop, a juggler, a bowling outing, and a boat trip down the river.

Fantastic Features

A day-care provider in one community expanded her program to include six school-agers. Each week one family was in charge of "Fantastic Features," which ran for approximately eight hours either in one day or in two half-day sessions. Each activity required one or two adults—either the parents, who took time off from work, or a friend who substituted. All activities had to last for an extended period of time and to be integrated into the daily program. Fantastic Features included the following events:

- Gifts: creating friendship bracelets, potholders, and beading.

- A canoe trip: planning and going on the trip, and making books about their adventure.

- A bird station: making different kinds of feeders and houses and going to a local bird sanctuary.

- The world of photography: reviewing the techniques of taking good pictures, doing some creative photography, making pinhole cameras, exploring animation, and going to a photo shop.

Family Night

Three families, with a total of nine children, took turns selecting and scheduling appropriate events every Thursday night. One family, for example, selected a free band concert; another bought ingredients to make pizza; and another arranged a fishing trip.

Nights Out

Four kids in a neighborhood got together twice a week for three hours in the evening. They took tennis lessons on one night and learned to use a sewing machine on the other. An adult with expertise took charge of each activity. During the week, in their spare time, the kids practiced their tennis and worked on their sewing projects, which included doll clothes and stuffed animals.

Chapter 4

Exploring Family Adventures

An occasional change of pace will help your child stay interested and involved in regular summer activities. Family outings and celebrations are good ways to break the routine. For getaways, some families prefer several short excursions; others would rather pack up and go somewhere for a longer stay. Excursions and vacations can be active or laid back, or they can combine raucous fun with time for relaxation.

In any case, be sure to plan ahead and see that each member of the family has a chance to do his or her own thing. If kids help plan the trip—from a weeklong vacation to a simple excursion—

they will feel more involved and be less likely to pester you about when you're leaving, when you're coming back, or whether you're almost there.

VACATIONS

A vacation is a perfect time for family members to enrich their lives and to grow together. On a vacation, parents and children can discover new parts of themselves and learn more about subjects and places. Whole families can learn to canoe or sail or can try silversmithing, gardening, or basket making.

A good family vacation will interest everyone on the trip. When planning, consider each person's needs, likes, and dislikes, starting with your youngest child and working up. Involve children in deciding where to go and what to do and in determining a general level of activity or relaxation. Plan days around everyone: kids shouldn't have to spend hours at museums, and parents shouldn't have to live at the amusement park.

A good way to get the whole family involved in planning is to have each member describe his or her dream vacation: Where would you go? What would you do? Chart these ideas, and then discuss what's realistic and what choices would keep the most family members happy. You may want to investigate in advance whether the place you are going has activities especially for children. If not, plan to bring favorite activities with you. If you need to cut costs, check with hotels and attractions for special deals.

Remember long drives can be difficult for youngsters. If your destination is more than two hours away, consider having a fun activity or overnight break between stretches of travel. Be sure to bring along a few exciting books for everyone to read in a car, train, or plane. Colored string for making friendship bracelets, gimp for making lanyards, travel games, and music for sing-alongs can also break the tedium.

Don't force children to spend every waking moment with the family. Find other kids for them to spend time with (this can be good for you, too), take turns with a spouse in being with children, or let children go off under other adult supervision.

Be realistic. You won't be able to see and do everything. Also, be flexible and open to new plans. The goal is to minimize disagreements and maximize fun.

Consider combining some of the following components to create a vacation everyone will enjoy.

- Visit a faraway grandparent to celebrate a birthday.

- Try canoeing, kayaking, hiking, cycling, or white-water rafting.

- Camp at a local campground, or take a longer trip to a national park or nature preserve. If you visit a state or national park, be sure to call ahead to local tourism bureaus for information.

- Go on a cruise or a boat ride.

- Stay on a farm or a dude ranch.

- Tour a major city, such as Boston, Washington, or San Francisco, or visit a historical place, such as Williamsburg.

- Take a sports-oriented vacation, in which everyone can play tennis, play golf, or sail, for example.

- Visit an adventure or a theme park.

EXCURSIONS

If you don't have time to travel far this summer or if you can't afford a big trip, explore your own community. Even a brief excursion can break your summer routine and be full of discovery, excitement, and surprises. Excursions with other families or groups of friends, even if only downtown or for an hour's drive into the country, can be adventurous. Summer excursions are your child's passport to new places and different worlds. Bring along a camera so you can add to your family photo album.

Discover different neighborhoods. Learn about new restaurants, ice cream shops, and historical sites. Trace the history of the city through photos and newspapers; study its water, sewer, and electrical systems. Consider visiting town merchants and civil servants to learn how the city operates. Visit some of your town's popular tourist destinations. Find a safe place to meet out-of-town tourists and find out why they come to visit. Drive to a new part of town and take a walk. Cap off the day by putting questions on index cards to make a trivia game about your town or community.

Following are more ideas for one-day or brief family excursions.

Go to an ethnic grocery store: Chinese, Korean, Greek, Hispanic, Indian, or other. See how many new foods your children can find. Ask the proprietor about some of the foods that interest you. At the end of the day, prepare a meal from the culture you have explored, or eat at an ethnic restaurant.

Attend an outdoor concert. Many towns and communities offer free outdoor summer concerts. Children can learn about composers or musical styles. Relax with a picnic supper, or take an exotic treat with you.

Sleep in a new place. Take a minivacation at a nearby hotel or motel. When you make reservations, be sure to ask if there's a swimming pool or a game room. Have a picnic on the way, or order a meal from room service. Watch a video together to top off the adventure. Consider camping out in your own backyard. Preparations can take several days, as each child packs, prepares snack foods, makes up a scary ghost story to tell by flashlight, and puts together the stuff to build a camp-fire. Other possibilities would be to send your child to sleep over at a friend's house or to have the whole family "camp" in one person's room.

Make new friends. Find out if your local humane society allows the public to play with the animals. If appropriate, explain to your child before you go that you are only visiting the animals (as you would at a zoo) and will not be bringing one home.

Visit a country fair. Familiarize children with various competitions, and observe what entries—by children and adults—have won prizes. Learn about livestock shows, carnival rides, and exhibits. Encourage children to enter a competition, such as baking, sewing, arranging flowers, or raising animals.

Take your child to work. No matter where you work, your child will be interested. Conversations on the way to and from work, lunch at a local cafeteria, meetings with your colleagues, and the machinery and equipment will all provide stimulation, excitement, and learning.

Jocelyn, age nine, has been visiting her father's printing shop regularly for the past four years. By stacking the paper bins, she learned the names of dozens of subtle colors: aquamarine, carnation pink, and others. Jocelyn enjoyed inventing her own names such as vomit yellow. As she learned to spell, she made rubber stamps. Her first "professional" job was making tags for her school fair.

Explore other workplaces. Plants, farms, and factories in your area may have scheduled tours or be willing to set up something for a group. Ask people you know who work in interesting fields if they would take your child or a small group of children on a behind-the-scenes tour of their workplace. Following are several possible destinations.

- A newspaper. Visit the newsroom, layout area, and printing presses.

- An assembly line. Watch cars being made.

- An amusement park. Try the new water slide.

- A toy factory. Watch the production of games, trucks, or dolls.

- A costume company.

- A candy store. See chocolate being melted, molded, wrapped, and packed.

- A secondhand shop, auction, or estate sale. See old clothes, books, toys, furniture, and trinkets.

- A farm. Learn about raising and breeding animals and about planting and harvesting crops.

- A local television, radio, or cable station.

- The state house. Watch legislators debate, see the governor's office, or ask a clerk to explain how a bill becomes a law.

- An experimental station. See how hybrid varieties of flowers and vegetables are tested and rated.

- A post office. Look for stamp collections depicting a variety of interests.

- The division of Fisheries and Wildlife. Visit hatcheries where rainbow trout, brook trout, or other species are raised for stocking brooks and streams.

- Natural wildlife preserves.

- A U.S. Coast Guard station.

- A local lake or river. Canoe and hike. Bring along a picnic lunch.

- A local police or fire station.

- A nature center or petting zoo.

- A restored village. See how life was in earlier centuries.

- A boat trip. Go island hopping or whale watching.

CELEBRATIONS

Over the course of the summer, you may want to start some family traditions: a weekly bike ride in the country or an ice-cream parlor date, for example.

The five members of the Elliot family took turns selecting and scheduling important events for one family night each week. One week, Mrs. Elliot arranged for the family to build a bookshelf. She bought the materials, and on Friday night, the entire family helped cut, nail, sand, and stain the shelf. For his week, Mr. Elliot chose a funny play for the family to read aloud. Paula, thirteen, made arrangements to attend a free concert on the town common. Ten-year-old Adam found a recipe for pizza and bought ingredients; the family then prepared the pizza and ate it while watching part of a television miniseries on World War II. Eric, six, asked his mother to help him arrange for the family to dine at an Italian restaurant in a neighboring city. Each week, one member contributed creative ideas and the whole family looked forward to the night together.

Summer holidays make good starting points for celebrations and discovery. For Flag Day, June 14, for example, your kids could learn about different countries and the United Nations and make flags of many nations to decorate your house. Here are a few other ideas.

Celebrate summer history. Go to your library and find *Chase's Annual Events* (published yearly), which lists most types of events and observances across the country, including presidential proclamations, sponsored events, astronomical phenomena, historic anniversaries, folkloric events, famous birthdays, religious observances, and local events. For example, the directory points out that the week ending on the fourth Sunday in June is Amateur Radio Week; the melody to "Happy Birthday to You" was composed by Mildred J. Hill on June 27, 1859; and June 19, 1978, is the birthday of the popular comic-strip cat Garfield. Build projects and activities around the history you uncover. Your child will be fascinated by this unusual resource.

Help your kids organize a Fourth of July parade. They could begin by talking to other kids and adults in your neighborhood. Have them make signs to announce the event and decorate bikes, carts, or strollers with streamers, kites, balloons, and flags. Dolls, teddy bears, and pets can also "march" in the parade.

Involve everyone in making balloon animals (with environmentally safe balloons), blowing bubbles, and playing carnival games. Plan to end the parade at a location where everyone can eat and enjoy outdoor games.

Celebrate Beatrix Potter's birthday. On July 6, have a tea party and read some stories aloud to your child to celebrate the birthday of the author of *The Tale of Peter Rabbit*. Have your child write and illustrate a short book about your family's pet or some other animal and then read it aloud to the family. Use sheets of paper folded in half, with a piece of construction paper for the cover. Visit a nearby pet shop and pet the rabbits and other animals.

Honor the birthday of Henry David Thoreau. Thoreau, a U.S. writer born on July 12, 1817, believed people should be able to act based on their beliefs about right and wrong. In 1845, Thoreau moved to Walden Pond, near Concord, Massachusetts, where he built his own cabin and recorded his observations of nature. To celebrate Thoreau's birthday, have kids take a nature walk and record the things they see. They could begin keeping personal journals and learn how to make a book, collect wildflowers and dry or press them to preserve them, or design a game using rainforest animals.

For a special treat, celebrate the birth of the ice-cream cone. The cone was created on July 23, 1904, in St. Louis, Missouri, by a waffle vendor who decided to serve ice cream in rolled-up waffles. Help your kids make their own ice cream and, if they're ambitious, their own cones.

VANILLA ICE CREAM

Ingredients

4 eggs	1 qt whole milk
1³/₄ c sugar	3 trays crushed ice
1¹/₂ tsp vanilla extract	5 lb rock salt
¹/₄ tsp salt	topping, any kind
1 c evaporated milk	

Procedure

Have ready a large bowl, a mixing spoon, a pitcher, a 2-lb coffee can with a plastic lid, and a 1-gal plastic bucket.

1. Beat the eggs in the large bowl. Add sugar, vanilla, and salt.
2. Add milks. Stir until the mixture is smooth.
3. Pour the mixture into the pitcher and refrigerate overnight.
4. Pour the mixture into the coffee can until the can is half full. Cover the can with its plastic lid.
5. Place a layer of ice in the bottom of the bucket. Pour rock salt over the ice.
6. Place the can in the bucket. Pack layers of salt and ice around the can. Do not cover the top with ice.
7. Turn the can around and around in the bucket.
8. As the ice melts, add more ice and salt. Make sure no water gets into the coffee can.
9. After turning for about 10 minutes, wipe the residue from the plastic lid. The ice cream should be starting to freeze. Continue turning the can until the mixture is completely frozen.
10. Remove the ice cream from the can. Serve with your favorite topping (chocolate chips,

blueberries, coconut, raspberries, peaches, nuts, strawberries, cookie chunks, crushed candy bars, or anything else you want to try).

WAFFLE CONE

Ingredients

$1/4$ c butter, melted and cooled	$3/4$ c powdered sugar, sifted
2 egg whites, stiffly beaten	$1/8$ tsp salt
$1/4$ tsp vanilla	$1/2$ c flour

Procedure

Have ready a waffle iron and two bowls.

1. Preheat the waffle iron to medium.
2. In one bowl, fold the butter into the egg whites. Add the vanilla.
3. In a separate bowl, combine the powdered sugar, salt, and flour.
4. Gently fold the dry ingredients into the butter mixture.
5. Pour 1 tsp of batter into the waffle iron.

Heat each side to a golden beige, about 90 seconds.

6. Lift the wafer from the iron and shape into a cone. Allow cone to cool before filling.

Observe Mexican festivals. Throughout July, Mexicans celebrate with fairs, bullfights, fireworks, and sporting competitions. Rodeos, events that display fancy horsemanship, and dances, including the Mexican Hat Dance (the national dance), are all part of the fun. To share in these celebrations, kids could make spicy Mexican treats such as Mexican hot chocolate, tacos, and guacamole. They could design bright, colorful masks and costumes for dancing and learn several new dances. Or get a book on the origin of piñatas, make a piñata and fill it with goodies, and have a celebration to break open the piñata.

Enjoy the Perseids. On the Night of the Shooting Stars (usually August 12–13), people all over the world watch the annual meteor shower that seems to come from the constellation Perseus. Although each meteor may be as tiny as a grain of sand, observers see as many as sixty meteors an hour, and together they light up the sky brilliantly as they enter Earth's atmosphere. Children can celebrate the Perseids by having a campfire late at night and watching the sky. Roast marshmallows over the campfire, and make s'mores of roasted marshmallow and a chocolate bar between graham crackers. Build models of the constellations, write ghost stories to share after dark, and play flashlight tag after the show of shooting stars.

Chapter 5

· · · · · · · · · · · · · · · ·

Developing the Other Rs through Activities

Children spend much of the school year developing their skills in the three traditional Rs: reading, 'riting, and 'rithmetic. Summer is perfect for focusing on the other Rs: resourcefulness and risk taking, responsibility, and relationships. No matter what your child's particular interests, she or he can develop these other Rs through new experiences, reading, guided television and video viewing, computer fun, and summer safety. Acquiring new skills, developing competence, and having fun can go hand in hand as children explore new environments, new activities, new roles, new crafts, new tastes, and new hobbies.

Mastery of the first of the other Rs, resourcefulness and risk taking, means being able to

- look for something useful and interesting to do alone.

- maintain interest in an activity for an extended period.

- solve problems alone.

- deal with new situations and difficulties.

- take chances to reach important goals.

- have enough self-confidence to make decisions.

- accept both positive and negative aspects of a situation or experience.

- say, "I did it myself!"

A child who is responsible can

- take care of herself and her things.

- take care of others.

- take care of animals, plants, and the household.

- share or teach knowledge or skills.

- explain new ideas, experiences, or situations.

- complete assigned tasks.

- follow schedules and plans.

- pay attention and remember.

- trust and be trustworthy.

A child who understands relationships

- plays and interacts effectively with others.

- recognizes her own thoughts and feelings and those of others.

- observes the actions of himself and others.

- portrays the thoughts, feelings, and actions of real and imaginary persons in various situations.

- expresses her needs.

- is sensitive to others' needs.

LEARNING THROUGH NEW EXPERIENCES

Following are some activities that your child can do alone or that you can do as a family to help your child develop the other Rs. Use these as a starting point, and mix and match them over time. Note experiences that are most enjoyable for each child and for the family as a whole.

Environments

Children who create an environment of their own discover and explore a world they can understand and enjoy. Through comparison and contrast, they can better understand the "real world." Making a play space—whether a fort, clubhouse, tree house, or backyard store—can occupy children for hours at a time. If you don't have time to help, find a high school student who does. If the structure is permanent, the children will return to it over days, weeks, or even months, adding new features and decorations.

Sean and his best friend, Dan, built a fort out of two refrigerator boxes and played in the fort for several weeks during the summer. The fort had a clock, a place to eat, and a sign, and the boys painted it. They'd eat their lunch there and spend hours fixing up the place.

Building a play space can be as easy as putting together two boxes, or it can be much more complicated. One summer, several families collaborated to build five play areas over a period of ten weeks, giving children a chance to play and imagine all over the community.

Don't think that your child needs a backyard to create a new environment. Sitters will sometimes take kids to their homes to play, or a neighbor might share space. If all else fails, your child may use a porch or a public park. Any small open area will do. The space will be as interesting and as large as your child imagines it to be.

Following are some suggestions for creating a new environment.

Build a clubhouse or fort. Use boxes or blankets and a clothesline. If an adult can help, consider using tires, buckets, ropes, utility spools, wooden crates, bricks, blocks, boards, barrels, and furniture. Use a fold-up tent as a cave or secret hiding place. If you use bricks or other potentially hazardous materials, be sure the structure is absolutely safe before letting children play around it.

When kids tire of the fort or clubhouse, they can use most of the materials for an obstacle course. They can crawl through barrels, hop over tires, climb ropes, or balance on boards. (Check for nails or sharp edges!) Once the course is safe, children can learn about time and stopwatches by timing their runs.

Set up an invention center. Supply the center with tools your children know how to use and with scrap wood, rope, rods, pulleys, gears, building blocks, and so on. Rummage through your basement and closets for items that children could use for inventions. Visit a local junkyard or the town dump to look for treasures: old bicycles, typewriters, and other machines that can be taken apart. Consider buying kits for projects that your child can work on over time. Kits are available for working with solar energy, crystal radios, electro-magnetics, clocks, newspapers, or weather stations—just to name a few.

Make a backyard playground. Gather balls, bean-bags, marbles, jacks, chalk, Hula-Hoops, jump ropes, and a flashlight, and put them in a big "outdoors" box. Include at least some things one child can enjoy alone. Help children make up a list of outdoor games, such as tag, hide-and-seek, kick ball, and flashlight tag.

Set up an art studio. An outdoor art area can give birth to all sorts of exciting creative endeavors. Gather chalk, crayons, paints, paper of various colors, different-sized brushes, and materials for making whistles, rattles, and bells. Expand the area with materials for making mosaics, sculpture, and hand puppets. The outdoors is a good place for messy projects like tie-dyeing, batik, sand painting, or sculpting with papier-mâché, soap, or wood. Or try foot painting: On a sidewalk or other safe, flat surface, spread long strips of butcher paper. Mix diluted tempera paints in pie tins and set the kids to work—no hands allowed! The project can get slippery, so be sure kids can hold onto a fence or railing.

Put together a costume box and theater space. Visit a local thrift shop or Goodwill store to buy used clothing, uniforms, hats, and so on. Purses, scarves, and jewelry can also be fun. Don't forget to include a mirror.

If your children want to put on a magic show, get a book on simple magic tricks. Buy a deck of cards and help children make up some tricks. Many kids like to design magician hats, choose costumes, and make up silly names for themselves. After children have practiced with new props, let them put on a show for the whole family or group of friends.

Find material for making animal masks, African masks, and theater masks, or try papier-mâché. Children can create a variety of costumes and put on a play. Help them build a simple platform with curtains for performances. Or hold a masquerade lunch party and create animal- and clown-face sandwiches. Decide who wants to be a queen, a scary monster, a giant gorilla, or a cat, and ask kids why they chose what they did.

Build a puppet theater. If your children show an interest in getting or making hand puppets, find a large cardboard box and some makeshift curtains to create a stage. A group of children can make up plays and put them on for their families. For variety, turn the puppet stage into a police station, a restaurant, a concert hall, a specialty store, or a photography shop. Let your children and their friends define and redefine the box.

Discoveries

Take advantage of the natural curiosity of middle childhood. The following activities will spark or build on your child's wonder about the world, both natural and human-made.

Plant a tree—or count tree rings. Find a place in your yard or in your community where children can plant a tree. Help children research the area and learn what kind of tree would grow best there. You can get free seedlings with a ten-dollar membership in the National Arbor Day Foundation. (For more information, write to the foundation at 100 Arbor Avenue, Nebraska City, Nebraska 68410.) On another day, hike to the nearest tree stump and try to figure out how old the tree was when it was cut. The distance between each ring shows the tree's yearly growth. See if you can figure out which years were driest.

Forecast the weather. Help children keep track of the weather each day in a notebook or journal. Read up on the weather, and learn about different kinds of clouds and how to recognize them. Try to predict the weather for the next day. If possible, visit a local television or radio weatherperson to learn how he or she predicts the weather.

Become a nature lover. Design a "Nature Nurturer" badge for you child to wear on a backpack or jacket. Cut an index card into any shape (such as a triangle, heart, or star) and decorate it with your nature slogan or logo (such as "I'm a Nature Nurturer" or "I ❤ Earth"). Children could start a vegetable, flower, or herb garden in your backyard or join a community garden. Go to the library to find projects that involve herb and plant lore. For example, with adult supervision, children could make their own insect repellent.

INSECT REPELLENT

Materials

2 c sesame oil	$^1/_2$ c dried rosemary
$^1/_4$ c dried sage	16 garlic cloves, fresh

Instructions

1. Combine all ingredients in a pan.
2. Bring the mixture to a boil.
3. Cook until it thickens.
4. Place the liquid in small jars.
5. Let it settle for 1 to 2 weeks.
6. Strain into sterilized containers.

Help children inlay paper with flowers; make perfumes and essential oils from lavender and other herbs; make dyes from plants, and dye shoelaces, socks, and pillowcases; dry local plants, and make an identification chart, including locations and uses; weave a wreath of culinary herbs that can be hung in the kitchen and used for cooking; learn which herbs repel moths, and make sachets to store with sweaters; and/or make potpourri. (See the resources section for activity books that will explain how to make these things.)

Go stargazing. With your children, study a star chart before going outside. Go out on a clear, moonless night, and try to get away from lighted homes or cities. Take a compass, binoculars, or a telescope if you have one. Back inside, help children locate on the chart the constellations you saw, and record them. Read about the myths behind the names of the constellations, or have children draw them. (Kids love glow-in-the-dark stars attached to the ceiling.) On July 20, the anniversary of the first moon landing, have kids make astronaut puppets, read about the Apollo space missions, and eat "space food."

Focus on flight. On a nice day, help your kids make their own rocket launcher, build a kite, or make a balloon rocket (see directions, following). Make sandwiches in the shapes of airplanes, and test different kinds of paper airplanes. To end the day, rent a video about flying, such as *The Rocketeer* or *Radio Flyer*. Good books about flight include *Amelia Earhart: Flying for Adventure* (Houghton Mifflin); *Anne Morrow Lindbergh: Pilot and Poet* (Lerner Publications); and *The Glorious Flight: Across the Channel with Louis Blériot* (Puffin Books). Celebrate Anne Morrow Lindbergh's birthday (June 22) or National Aviation Day, commemorating Orville and Wilbur Wright's historic flight on August 19, 1903, at Kitty Hawk, North Carolina.

ROCKET LAUNCHER

Materials

¹/₂ c water	paper streamers
¹/₂ c vinegar	cork
1 qt plastic soda	1 tsp baking soda
bottle, empty	4" x 4" paper towel
thumbtack	

Instructions

1. This activity should be done with an adult!
2. Bring all materials to a wide outdoor space.
3. Pour the water and vinegar into the empty soda bottle.
4. Tack the paper streamers to the cork.
5. Put the baking soda on the paper towel, roll up the towel, and twist the ends closed.
6. Have an adult drop the paper towel into the bottle, and put the cork on as tightly as possible.
7. Stand back, and watch the cork rocket take off.

Balloon Rocket

Materials

string	twist tie
drinking straw	tape
balloon	

Instructions

1. Stretch a long piece of string across a room. Run it through a drinking straw before securing it tightly at both ends.
2. Blow up a balloon, and tie the end with a twist tie. Tape the body of the balloon to the straw so that the tied end of the balloon faces one end of the straw.
3. Slide the straw and balloon to one end of the string, untie the twist tie, and let the rocket go.
4. Experiment with different-sized balloons, add wings or a tail, measure the distance traveled by each rocket, and so on.

Learn about different modes of transportation. Take a ride on every form of transportation you can find, and learn how to use mass transit in your city or town. Look for places you and your child can visit by bus, boat, trolley, streetcar, train, or truck. Keep your ticket stub (if there is one) and a brochure or description of the transportation system. Learn about different sources of energy for transportation: gasoline, alternative fuels, solar power, wind power, and foot power.

Draw maps of your community. Using butcher paper, pencils, crayons, or markers, draw a map of your neighborhood, making the streets wide enough for toy vehicles. Laminate your map by pressing it between sheets of clear kitchen wrap. Help your child locate neighbors' houses and local landmarks such as trees, stores, and schools. Then take a "drive." On a smaller scale, make a version of Monopoly using the streets of your town. Or xerox several copies of a local map and make your own legend: color in friends' houses, parents' workplaces, routes to and from school and other activities, and other important landmarks.

Have a scavenger hunt. Divide neighborhood kids into teams. Make lists of items, and give each team a map of the area and a bag. Items might include, for example, odd words on signs, feathers, ticket stubs, acorns, a heart-shaped rock, pine cones, buttons, or bows. Afterward, let the kids talk about the treasures they found, indicating on the map where they found them.

Roles

Summer is a great time for children to try out new roles and take on new responsibilities. For instance, kids can practice their math skills and learn to make change for customers while earning money. As they earn their own pocket money, they learn about expenses and income and about supply-and-demand economics. Some kids may choose to donate what they've earned to a good cause.

Become "Captain Recycling." Children in their middle childhood begin to feel a passionate interest in the environment and its preservation. They will be intrigued to learn that each ton of paper recycled saves about seventeen trees. If you don't already recycle, ask about drop-off centers near your home. Let children sort and classify your recyclable materials. They could use plastic bins or cardboard boxes to create recycling bins for metal, glass, plastic, and newspapers. (Some communities provide bins and/or pickup service; call your town hall for information.) Help your child lead a walk around your yard or neighborhood to collect recyclable trash. Learn how to recycle your own paper. Pick up a paper-making kit or get some directions for making paper using two coffee tins, certain types of screens, and wood. Use the recycled paper to make a book with pictures and stories of summer activities. (You could also make ink from some types of nonpoisonous berries.) Papier-mâché also recycles paper. Children can learn to make plates, bowls, jewelry, toys, boxes, and more and then sell the items or give them as presents.

Take over the kitchen night. Let your kids use simple cookbooks, such as *Pretend Soup* (Tricycle Press), to create a menu for dinner. With appropriate adult supervision, they could try a different combination of recipes each week. Children could make a sign, menus, and place mats with the name or logo of their "restaurant." They could decorate the kitchen table with a tablecloth and candles. Let your child handle all the safe parts of cooking a meal, serving it, and cleaning up. You can play the role of the snooty customer!

You might want to visit different restaurants for ideas on creating new dishes. Or post some of these fun recipes on your refrigerator so the kids can try them.

CITRUS SODA

Ingredients

juice of 1 lemon, lime, or orange	1 tsp sugar
	1 tsp baking soda
1 glass water	ice cubes

Procedure

1. In a glass, mix freshly squeezed juice with water and sugar.
2. Add baking soda. Stir until bubbly.
3. Add ice cubes. Drink.

YOGURT POPS

Ingredients

yogurt, any flavor	Popsicle or similar
pop molds or paper cups	sticks

Procedure

1. Pour yogurt into molds or paper cups.
2. Place one stick in each mold or cup.
3. Freeze for 3 to 4 hours.
4. Remove pops from molds or peel off the paper cups. Enjoy.

BANANARAMA

Ingredients

banana	$1/4$ c peanuts or
plastic fork	almonds, crushed
$1/2$ c plain or vanilla yogurt	

Procedure

1. Cut the banana in half. Insert the fork in the flat end of the banana.
2. Cover with yogurt.
3. Coat with crushed nuts.
4. Freeze until firm.
5. Remove carefully. Enjoy.

Open a lemonade stand. Have a child invite some neighborhood friends to work on this project. With some guidance, the kids can decide what to make and sell: lemonade, fruit punch, Popsicles, bags of snack food, and so on. Children will enjoy designing and building the stand, creating posters to advertise their business, and preparing the treats.

Adopt a pet. Let your child select a pet—even something as small as a turtle. Read all about the pet before it arrives, and decide on its care and feeding. Visit a zoo or aquarium, and go to the library or bookstore to find books about the animal. If you can't purchase a pet, collect pictures and stuffed animals. If you have agreed to pet-sit for a vacationing friend, ask your child to help.

Care for a younger child. Older children can blossom when they take on the responsibility of caring for a younger sibling, relative, or neighbor for a few hours a day or week. They learn about child-rearing and relish the trust others place in them. If your child is a new baby-sitter, you or another adult will want to be available to give help and advice.

Zander, age twelve, was offered the opportunity to baby-sit five-year-old Craig, who lived in his apartment building. Zander's mother helped him shop for snacks for Craig, suggested activities, and helped him purchase several activity books. Zander began to understand the importance of planning so that Craig would not be bored. Although Zander's parents had to be "on call" when Zander baby-sat, they encouraged him to take the job, demonstrating to him the importance they placed on caring for children and their confidence that he could do it.

Publish a community newsletter. Have children divide the news into "beats," or areas of interest: local sporting events, movie reviews, interviews with local celebrities about what they do or with old-timers about the town's history, and comic strips. Use a desktop publishing program, and print or xerox copies. Establish subscriptions and delivery routes, and try to publish at least once a month.

Have a toy sale. Ask neighborhood children to look for toys they never use or have outgrown. Children can design posters to advertise the sale, decide on prices, and run the sale. They could also create an illustrated catalog with humorous descriptions of items for sale.

Run a neighborhood Olympics. Kids can organize and run events such as the sponge toss, shooting hoops, a sack race, a pitching contest, the yard dash, a high jump, a long jump, and an around-the-house relay. Decide on prizes in advance. Castoff, but still appealing, toys and costumes make good choices.

A great event for the Olympics is "pack your bag." Stuff a suitcase with old clothes and place it at one end of the yard. Players line up at the other end. At the command "go," the players race across the yard, open the suitcase, and dump out the clothes. As the clothes tumble out, the kids grab garments and put them on over the clothing they are already wearing. They put on as many pieces as they can—hats, mittens, shirts, ties, and anything else they can find. The round ends when players are wearing every article of clothing; players get one point for each item they are wearing. Play until one person reaches eleven points. Then put the clothes back in the suitcase and begin the next round.

Enter a contest. Find a contest that relates to your child's interest, or set up your own. Most school-agers will find something they'll enjoy in *All the Best Contests for Kids* (Ten Speed Press)—whether their talent is in art, music, theater, photography, reading, writing, math, science, or pig calling. Or your child could find a place to publish a story, poem, or picture.

Host a crafts fair. Suggest that each child make a certain number of objects to sell using whatever crafts he or she enjoys most: cards, jewelry, potholders, origami, lanyards, papier-mâché, pottery, and so on. Take a trip to a crafts-supply store for materials; have the kids keep track of what they spend. Set aside several craft days for the children to create the work they're planning to sell. Then advertise and hold a fair.

If your kids are tired of the crafts they know, help them try some of the following ideas.

Create colorful place mats. Paste cutout phrases and pictures from used greeting cards, newspapers, or magazines onto a poster board. Laminate it.

Make picture frames. Use two pieces of cardboard the same size; cut out the center of one piece. Decorate the border using paints, markers, or torn pieces of tissue. Glue the picture to the solid piece of cardboard, and glue the border on top.

Weave wall hangings. Tie several twelve- to eighteen-inch pieces of yarn between two pieces of wood. Using this as a loom, weave dried grasses, corn husks, reeds, branches of dried berries, feathers, shells, ribbons, fabric, or other objects into each piece of yarn.

Put on a performance. Have kids produce a puppet show, an original play, a variety show with music, dancing, magic tricks, and so on. A variety show could also include short skits based on the kids' experiences and/ or on their favorite characters from books and movies. The children may want to build a puppet theater or a stage with sets or design costumes and programs. Each child could design a certain number of programs: all would contain the same information but reflect the style of the artist. The kids may also want to design fancy tickets. Kids who don't want to perform could take tickets, usher, raise curtains, and operate spotlights. Advertise the performance in the neighborhood and charge a nominal fee, just enough to make the kids feel like they've created a real show.

Do summer chores. Most kids rank chores among their "most hated" things to do. In fact, chores are probably the cause of more grumbling and family arguments than anything else. Even so, in most families, everybody pitches in. Families that don't need much help from children still assign appropriate tasks, putting their kids in charge of themselves and their things. Giving kids chores means giving them responsibility, which helps them understand how your family works and how they fit into it. Only you can decide what chores are appropriate for your children, but here are some suggestions for getting your kids excited about chores.

❖ Identify and list all chores that need to be done on a daily, weekly, or other basis. The list should include some chores for each member of your family.

❖ Select appropriate chores to assign each child. Make sure children understand, and are able to do, the tasks assigned.

❖ Create a reminder system that is fun to use. Kids enjoy chores more if they can keep track of them with stickers or markers. When children see how their efforts fit into the family setting, they feel more in control and less a victim of other family members' demands.

❖ Allow children a reasonable amount of time to complete chores.

- Give positive feedback. Frequent words of praise are enough for some kids, but others do better with treats as rewards. Try giving coupons for movies or trips to the zoo.

- Don't view children as free labor. If your child is watching TV, reading a book, or just relaxing, don't ask for immediate help.

SUMMER READING

Kids find reading to themselves exhilarating. They feel independent, because they don't have to wait until you're free to read aloud to them, and they can choose their own books, magazines, comic strips, and so on. The ability to read opens the whole world of books to children, but that isn't all. Suddenly, notes from parents are clear, and so are signs on buildings and streets, and charts and diagrams. Things like telephones, typewriters, and computers make sense. Parents often notice a leap in independence soon after children begin reading to themselves.

Gwen started to read at the age of five. Immediately Rose, Gwen's mother, felt less pressure to find something for her daughter to do. When Gwen received a toy that required assembly, she asked Rose to help her put it together. Rose was busy and said she would help shortly. By the time she went to help Gwen, the child had read the directions and put the toy together herself. She was already playing with it!

Most children who read have parents who read. If your children see you engrossed in a book, magazine, or newspaper or hear you talking about something you have read, they learn that reading is part of growing up. Research shows that children often develop lifelong reading habits between ages ten and twelve. These are also the years when children may have activities in which reading gets tougher because of smaller print and more complex concepts.

Other than making sure your children have access to all sorts of good reading material, reading aloud is the best thing you can do to help them read and appreciate books. Children love to be read to. Younger children learn the conventions of reading: how to hold a book, how to turn pages, and how to move sequentially through a book. Older children learn new words and expressions. Even if your children know how to read, they will get a sense of story and plot when you read to them that they can't get on their own. Learning the rhythms of storytelling will help your child be a better reader.

Kids love picture books, color photos, comic books, and other materials that teach them how to decode pictures. Understanding pictures helps kids understand letters and words. Even if you're worried about your child's first choices of reading materials, let well enough alone. A child's interest in reading is precious, so it is best to respect personal choices.

Following are some suggestions for encouraging summer reading.

- Set aside twenty minutes a day for reading. This is enough to turn your child into an excellent reader.

- Set aside a period of time for parents and children to read aloud.

- Organize reading materials so children can find what they're looking for. Arrange books by subject; keep magazines and reference books together.

- Subscribe to one or two magazines for your child. Children love to get mail, and they will read these over and over.

- For kids who don't care about reading, try *Asterix* and *Tintin* books. These densely illustrated books are great for drawing in children who are having difficulty getting started in reading.

- Explore mysteries. Read favorites such as Encyclopedia Brown books. Have children read stories aloud and then try to guess the solutions. Older kids may prefer Sherlock Holmes books. Find a passage in one of the stories where Holmes describes someone he's just met. Discuss the assumptions Holmes makes. Is he right?

- Send reading "care packages" to children at camp or at home.

- Read maps and travel brochures together when planning family trips and excursions.

- Encourage children to exchange letters, clippings, and photographs with friends made on vacation.

TELEVISION AND VIDEO VIEWING

Most children ages six to twelve tend to watch too much TV, although the kids themselves often deny this. To add to your worries, the shows kids watch are sometimes violent and frightening. Kids who watch four or five hours of television a day often have learning problems, restless behavior, and reading deficits. These children score lower on achievement tests than children who watch less television. If they are weaned (kicking and screaming) from television, their test scores and reading levels improve.

Most children shouldn't watch more than two hours of television a day. Setting limits on TV time, especially if your children are alone at home during the summer, is a continuing process. Furthermore, limits alone are not enough. Simply explaining that TV is bad will not help children become critical TV viewers. Talk about television with your children, who may not understand that not all of what they see on TV is real. Talk about stereo-types—in terms of race, class, and gender—to make sure that your children grow up with your family's values, not necessarily the values seen on television.

Discussing differences between TV and books can also help children become less interested in TV and more interested in reading. Point out that books happen in your head, while TV usually doesn't make you think. Ask children what they would change about TV if they could. How could TV be made more real? Consider your own viewing habits. What sort of example are you setting?

Following are some suggestions for critical television viewing.

- Use a television guide with your children to decide what shows to watch.

- Create a list of acceptable programs for each child, and update it regularly.

- Be clear about the amount of time your kids can watch each day. Make sure they understand that they cannot save up TV time.

- Keep an accurate log of exactly how many hours you and your children watch TV each week. Discuss whether you need to limit viewing time.

- Read aloud to your children instead of letting them watch TV.

Watching a video can be great fun for the whole family, especially on rainy days or when you're stuck indoors. Videos produced especially for children are available at many local libraries and video clubs. Try educational and instructional videos, cartoons, sing-alongs, and full-length features such as *Snow White and the Seven Dwarfs, Mary Poppins,* and *Pete's Dragon.* Be aware, though, that videos are not immune to the problems of television. Make sure your children understand and think about the roles they see on the screen.

Following are some suggestions for critical video viewing.

- Limit the time your children watch videos, in the same way you limit television. Restrict your children to two hours a day of television and video viewing combined.

- Choose videos appropriate to your child's age. Preview videos before your child watches them, or watch along with your child and discuss the program afterward.

- Pick videos that will hold your child's attention for repeated viewings, especially if you buy them. Keep your child's current interests in mind.

- Look for award-winning videos made specifically for children. *Family Circle,* the *Video Magazine, Video Librarian, Parenting,* and *Parents' Choice* review children's videos. Every quarter, *TV Guide* publishes a list of videos recommended for family viewing.

DEVELOPING COMPUTER LITERACY

Summer is a perfect time for children to explore and use educational software programs or on-line services. Some kids might even enjoy a one- or two-week computer camp sponsored by a club, vocational school, or museum. Creatively designed software and on-line services stimulate imagination and help children learn to read, write, think, analyze, reason, and solve problems. Children can work at their own pace, getting instant access and instant feedback.

All-Time Favorite Family Videos

101 Dalmatians
Aladdin
Angels in the Outfield
Anne of Green Gables
Babe
Babes in Toyland
Baby-Sitters Club Series
Bambi
Beauty and the Beast
Beethoven Series
Benji
Charlie and the Chocolate Factory
Charlie Brown's All-Stars
Charlotte's Web
Chitty Chitty Bang Bang
Cinderella
The Dark Crystal
Dennis the Menace
E.T.: The Extra-Terrestrial
Free Willy

Harriet the Spy
Hercules
Home Alone Series
Homeward Bound
The Jungle Book
Lady and the Tramp
The Lion King
Little Giants
The Little Mermaid
Mary Poppins
The Mighty Ducks
The Muppet Movie
Oliver & Company
The Parent Trap
Pete's Dragon
Peter Pan
Pinocchio
Pippi Longstocking
Pocahontas
Pollyanna

The Red Balloon
Rescuers Down Under
Rikki Tikki Tavi
The Secret Garden
Secret of NIMH
The Shaggy Dog
Short Circuit Series
Sleeping Beauty
Snoopy, Come Home
Snow White and the Seven
    Dwarfs
The Sound of Music
Star Wars Trilogy
The Thief and the Cobbler
Toy Story
The Wind in the Willows
The Wiz
The Wizard of Oz
Yellow Submarine
Zeus and Roxanne

Companies are striving to produce top-quality, easy-to-use, fun programs for children of all ages. Educational software includes tools for creative expression, drill and practice, and games and simulation. Children can learn—alone or with others—the basic skills of reading, writing, arithmetic, science, social studies, language skills, and interpersonal awareness. They can even learn music theory and how to design a rock video.

As children spend more time with computers, they watch less television. Parents need to monitor computer time as well, however. Computer video games may not be any more educational than television programs. Parents need to help their children choose software that stimulates the imagination and teaches. Good software has escalating levels of difficulty, focuses on the child's interests, and integrates educational content and entertainment. Parents should also be careful not to allow the computer to replace their own involvement in a child's education.

Matching software to the computer a child will be using can be tricky. You'll need the right operating system and accessories, such as an external speaker, to run any software you purchase. If you can't remember the relevant information about your computer, write it down. The software package should tell you what you need to run the program: the required operating system, the amount of RAM, a hard drive or a particular type of floppy-disk drive, a mouse, the type of graphics display, the kind of printer, any sound-enhancement device, and so on. If you buy graphics software, make sure you have a compatible printer; children may be disappointed if they can't print out their work. (Particularly when you get new software, set limits on the amount of printing children do.) If you and your child will share a computer, make sure the system is set up so that children can play without jeopardizing other programs on the machine.

If you already have a computer, consider purchasing a CD-ROM player. Multimedia programs now available include electronic encyclopedias, dictionaries, thesauruses, maps, photos, and teaching and learning tools that combine texts with voices, sound effects, illustrations, and directions. World Book's Information Finder is particularly good for children. Schools also use National Geographic Society's Mammals: A Multimedia Encyclopedia; The Presidents: It All Started with George; and Picture Atlas of the World.

Software is expensive. Consider creating a lending library with other families whose computers are compatible. Lending someone your software is legal; making a copy is not—just as lending a book to a friend is legal but copying the book and giving the friend the copy is illegal. Shareware is software that users can copy for a nominal fee; your local bookstore or library should have guides to available shareware, and computer bulletin boards may also be good sources of appealing programs.

Types of Software

In exploring the many kinds of software available, think about what may be most useful and interesting for your child.

Tools for Creative Expression

Word processors allow children to write efficiently. With this type of software, children can correct mistakes easily; manipulate words, sentences, and paragraphs; and format text. Some word processors also incorporate a spelling checker, a thesaurus, and other useful features. Because making corrections is easier, most children find writing compositions with a computer to be more rewarding. Many begin to enjoy writing and, in fact, write longer and more creative papers.

Database management systems, or filing systems, allow children to store and retrieve information. Children can typically manipulate information in different ways. They can sort alphabetically or numerically, for example, or update, edit, or print out an entire database or selected parts of it. Children can create and use files of their friends' addresses, birthdays, and phone numbers; books; places to visit in a city; or collections of baseball cards, stamps, or coins.

With graphics tools, children can create colorful, detailed drawings and store, change, or print the results or use them in other programs. Children can express themselves freely through this adaptable, responsive medium. Some programs even allow children to draw pictures using a stylus. The artist can change the thickness of the "brush," the texture of the chosen area, or the colors—or work on a magnified section of the drawing.

Music-making tools allow a child without previous music theory experience to create musical themes. A child can also write, save, play, and invent variations on original songs.

General-purpose programming languages help children learn logic and develop problem-solving skills. With instruction, children implement original ideas, take more direct control over the computer, and gain experience using logical and organizational skills.

Drill-and-Practice Software

Through drill and practice, children review already-learned skills—for example, arithmetic, such as addition, subtraction, and multiplication. Most of these programs display a problem on the screen and ask for an answer, usually a choice from several possibilities. The computer tells the child if the answer is correct. Spelling, foreign languages, geography, and history exercises are also available. Many such programs couch the actual drill in the form of a game: correct answers help the player advance on a quest for buried treasure, for example.

Games and Simulations

Computer games come in all forms. Some provide little opportunity for learning, while others are powerful, exciting, and educational. Many contend, for example, that the traditional arcade-type game has little educa-tional value. These games are exciting, though, and children love to play them just for fun.

At the other extreme are the games called simulations, in which children take a role in a simulated world, perhaps as explorer or detective. Children are actively involved in these games, which may have exciting sound effects, music, graphic scenery, and format but also teach facts such as state capitals. Children use creative reasoning or work cooperatively with a group to solve problems and learn to read and retain facts, take notes, and think analytically.

Selecting Appropriate Software

Ask around before purchasing software. Find out what your child's teacher recommends. Ask other parents what their children have enjoyed and learned from. Look for reviews in newsletters such as "Children's Software Revue" or in guidebooks (see resources section). Has the software won major awards for excellence given by groups such as Parents' Choice Awards and the Software Publishing Association?

Take a careful look at the software itself.

- Is the program easy for children to use? Are instructions, both in the manual and on-screen, clear and easy to follow? Can a child who is stuck get help? Does a child need specialized skills to succeed? Does the program make it easy to pause in the middle to take a break?

- Is the software age appropriate for the child? School-age and preschool children have different software needs. A program claiming to be appropriate for "ages four to adult" probably isn't. A program with an age range of four to six years is better. Find age ranges closest to the age of your child, as they will be the most effective.

- What is the content of the software? Is the program meaningful? Does the software relate to the child's interest and help develop a skill? Does it require frequent decisions and problem solving? What does it teach? What kind of thinking does the program encourage: problem solving, creative thinking, memorization? Don't rely on the description on the back of the package. Try the software out yourself, and have your children use it. Many stores have demonstration stations where children can experiment with programs. Allow enough time to test a program thoroughly. Will the program hold a child's interest over time?

- Is the content free of racial, sexual, cultural, and ethnic stereotypes? How does the program treat violence?

- Can the program adapt to a child's rapidly changing abilities and interests? Is it flexible? Does the program present new challenges as skill level increases? Does the program encourage children to create and solve their own problems, or does it offer only predesigned yes-or-no problems? Does the program address more than one goal or have multiple applications and uses?

- Who controls what happens in the program? Can the child decide which direction the program takes, or does the computer make all the decisions? Can the child choose to move to another speed or skill level, to exit, or to change the parameters of the program?

- How does the program respond to successes and errors? Children like software that responds encouragingly and energetically—with whistles, bells, or animation. When a child is stuck, does the program support continuing and figuring out things? Does the program help children learn, or does it provide immediate answers to problems?

❖ Does the program motivate, interest, and intrigue children? Does it continue to challenge the child who masters it? Can the child keep track of how well he or she does?

❖ Are the graphics, text, and sound well done, appropriate, and effective? Is the screen easy to read and understand? Can a child easily interact with and respond to the program? Do the component parts of the program—sound, color, animation, and so on—enhance or detract from the goals of the program?

On-Line Services

On-line services, available to people with modems, offer much to children: encyclopedias, clubs, games,

---

Popular Software for School-Age Children

The Amazon Trail

Animated Storybook Series

Carmen Sandiego Series

Creative Writer

Fine Artist

Kid Cuts

Kid Pix

Kid Works Series

The Magic Schoolbus Series

Math Blaster Series

My Own Stories

The Oregon Trail

Outnumbered

Print Shop Deluxe

Reader Rabbit Series

Sim City

Spellbound

Stickybear's Series

Storybook Weaver

Super Solvers, Gizmos & Gadgets

Treasure Mountain

Zoo Keeper

pen pals, instant messages, and more. CompuServe, America Online, and Prodigy, some of the largest providers of services, offer programs for children. Many of these services have low-cost introductory offers; be sure to find out the real hourly cost. If you decide to keep a service, you may want to limit the amount of time children spend on-line and discuss costs in advance. Services available on the Internet change almost daily, so check periodically to see what's around for children.

Most on-line service customers are adult, so be sure to find out whether the service provides policing and whether you can arrange to make certain "adult" discussion sessions off-limits to children. Explore available games and discussion groups to find out which are age appropriate for your children. Some imaginative role-playing games, for example, are designed for adults and include violence or other inappropriate scenarios. Discuss basic safety rules regarding interactions with people children "meet" via computer—similar to safety rules you've established for strangers met in person. Children should not give out your address, for example. Post rules near the computer for children to consult if awkward situations arise.

ENCOURAGING SUMMER SAFETY

Children try new things, visit new places, and spend some time alone in the summer. Teach your child to do these things safely.

The best way to teach summer safety is to involve children in a complete learning process. Talking and doing are both essential. Talk about possible dangers and ways to protect yourself. Consider your child's age, level of maturity, and environment. Practice for particular situations so that children will be better prepared if something goes wrong.

Talk frankly and often about safety. Listen patiently to your child's fears and concerns. What he fears is just as important as what you fear and sometimes children need to verbalize a fear to overcome it. When your child tells you that she's scared of a vacant lot or a monster in the basement, take her seriously. Investigate the fears together—maybe while holding hands—and deal with imagined dangers as well as real ones.

The way you approach a child's fears is important. Telling your child, in an authoritative voice, to stay away from strangers, with no further explanation, won't relieve fear or provide useful information. Think about it: Stay away from strangers! You haven't defined what a stranger is. Children might assume that a stranger is anyone they haven't been introduced to. Make sure you define words children might not understand. In this instance, suggest that your child ask himself these questions: Do I know this person's name? Have I seen this person before? Do I know what this person does in the community? Try role-playing to help children memorize questions. If the answer to all these questions is no, the person really is a stranger. Explain that a stranger might hurt a child or take a child away.

Talking about summer dangers can help your family come up with guidelines and procedures for dealing with potential safety problems and prepare your child to know how to act when problems arise.

Following are a few potential dangers:

❖ swimming accidents at pools, lakes, or beaches.

❖ hiking and camping mishaps: insect bites, poisonous plants, rashes.

❖ boating, water-skiing, or other sporting accidents.

❖ automobile, bike, or motorbike accidents.

❖ sunburn or sun poisoning.

❖ lightning and storm damage.

❖ fires from stoves, outdoor grills, fireworks, furnace, appliances, or matches.

❖ home accidents or injuries: cuts, burns, falls, choking, poisoning.

❖ problems with other people: crank phone calls, muggings, someone following a child home, a break-in at home or at a neighbor's house, strangers at the door, someone asking if a child's parents are home.

❖ problems outside the house: lost keys, a lost child, a stolen bike.

❖ fights with siblings or other children.

Some schools and community organizations offer safety programs that allow children to practice handling emergency situations. Some classes also teach basic first-aid skills, how to arrange time spent alone, or ways to cope with potential dangers and with fear. Investigate the options; children learn better in behavioral programs where they actively rehearse handling emergencies than in discussion groups where they stay seated. Help children adapt lessons to your own home, pointing out, for example, different escape routes in case of fire. Review safety procedures often. Even children who participate in safety programs forget safety skills after a few months.

Children's safety depends on preparation, practice, and discussion. If you discuss specific situations in advance, you and your children will have time to think about what they should do and come up with some family safety guidelines before problems occur. Think about safety issues in the following scenarios. What should children do in each situation? Have your children practice. Use the scenarios to generate some summer safety guidelines and rules, and post the rules where they can be reviewed easily.

Scenario 1

Your best friend is coming over on her bike to play computer games at your house. You look out the window and see your friend knocked off her bike by a moving car. What would you do?

Questions to Get You Started

- ❖ How would you get help?

- ❖ What would you do and say when you asked for help?

- ❖ What could you do to help your friend?

What You Can Do

- ❖ Get help from an adult right away. Before you leave the house, make sure you or someone else calls your local emergency number.

- ❖ Be aware of traffic in the street and your own safety before you run to your friend.

- ❖ Stay calm. Tell your friend that help is coming.

- ❖ Wait. Don't move your friend if she can't move herself.

- ❖ Keep her warm with a sweater or jacket if you can.

- Review the steps for making an emergency phone call.

- Make sure everyone in your family knows bike safety rules and wears bike helmets.

- Make sure children wear reflective patches or tape on clothing, bikes, and helmets. Remind your children to avoid biking at night.

Scenario II

You are making a craft project and want to finish in a hurry. To make the paint dry faster, you plug the dryer into a socket that's also being used for a clock radio, a lamp, and a coffeepot. Suddenly you notice sparks and smoke coming out of the socket. A little flame is starting to move down the cord. What would you do?

Questions to Get You Started

- Would you try to put out the fire?

- What would you do to keep it from getting worse?

- How would you get help?

What You Can Do

- Turn off the switches of all appliances, if possible. Leave the room immediately and close the door so that the fire doesn't spread.

- Leave the house and call the fire department from a neighbor's house.

Family Safety Tips

- Talk with your child about the proper use and hazards of electrical appliances and circuits. Never overload electrical outlets.

- Have a fire extinguisher and smoke alarm on each floor of your home. Teach everyone how and when to use them. Make sure your child knows to leave the building immediately if a fire is too big to handle.

- Talk with your child about what to do in case of fire. Be sure to review "stop, drop, and roll."

- Make sure everyone knows how to report a fire.

Safety Kit

Assembling a summer safety kit of emergency supplies can be a great way to help your children learn. Discuss each item as you put the kit together. Place items in a fanny pack, backpack, cassette box, jewelry box, or plastic egg. Update the kit regularly, refilling it and adding new items. The kit will provide children with a sense of security and help them develop a sense of independence and responsibility. You and your children can think of other helpful items, but you should consider including the following:

- change for emergency phone calls.

- money (in money holder) for emergency transportation.

- a medical insurance identification card.

- a key ring with keys to the house, bicycle locks, and so on.

- a list of phone numbers, including parents' workplaces, neighbors, relatives, family doctor, hospital, fire, and police.

- individual-sized containers of water or juices.

- nutritious snacks—even candy.

- pen, pencil with eraser, and pad of paper.

- small clock or watch.

- small flashlight (with extra batteries).

- small first-aid kit (with sterile bandages).

- games, toys, and books to use while waiting for parents, a cab, or a bus.

- a reassuring note: "I love you!"

Do not label the kit or keys or list your home telephone number. Refill and update the kit periodically, and be sure to keep telephone numbers current.

Together, you and your child can develop plans and habits that promote safety, whether you're together or apart for a while. Everyone will be more relaxed and confident about your child's independence once your family's safety rules and guidelines are understood.

Afterword

Treasuring Summer Memories

Throughout the summer, you and your children can celebrate wonderful events and activities as they happen and record them to look back on later. Preserving summer memories can help your child reflect periodically on how summer is going and perhaps get him thinking about activities he would like to try before summer is out. Think of the following projects and fun for rainy days or moments of boredom.

Diary

Encourage children to write whatever they wish. If they write even a few lines each day, they will be able to look back on what they've written with an enormous sense of accomplishment. At the end of each day, kids might describe one funny thing that happened that day—why it was "upside-down day" or "backward day," for example—or one unusual sight or experience. Suggest an "adventure notebook" to record all adventures and to plan more adventures for next summer—or a spy notebook like Harriet the Spy's. If your children spend much of the summer outdoors, they could record birds and animals spotted and wildflowers, trees, and mushrooms identified in a nature journal. They could also keep leaves, pressed flowers, and feathers there. Children may want to illustrate the diary with original pictures.

Encourage children to decorate the diary cover creatively. A diary should give a sense that the child is indeed the star. For variety, children could make the paper for the diary and write with a feather- or wood-nib pen, using ink made from blackberries, cherries, or raspberries. Atmospheric lettering, comic-strip lettering, graffiti styles, or handwriting styles would all make diary entries more exciting.

Travel journals also help children of this age group learn. Children frequently tell stories based on detailed, hand-drawn pictures and written descriptions of sights.

Audiotape or Videotape

If your child does not enjoy writing, have her keep a tape-recorded diary. She could record stories about fun times (a great picnic or a trip to the circus) or interesting ones (the time someone got lost on the boat trip or the night she saw a shooting star). In fact, the entire family could tape an oral history. Every family member has a story, a biography, a piece of family history worth telling and saving.

Videotapes capture the expressions and dimensions of people's personalities and are fun to make. During the summer, children might learn videotape techniques and how to conduct and edit interviews. They might use these skills to create a video record of the summer, perhaps including the family vacation, favorite backyard activities, events at camp, and other summer highlights. Or they might make a "documentary." For example, on summer holidays, like the Fourth of July, they could interview town residents about celebrations in their childhood and the origin of local traditions. Encourage children to make up questions to help focus the production. After watching it in the winter, consider ideas for another audio or video record to be made the following summer.

Photo Album or Scrapbook

Find a good how-to book and help your child explore photography. Learn all about using light, composing a photograph, and taking landscape, close-up, and action shots. Take photos of favorite events, places, friends, and special experiences, and collect them in an album; or use them to construct a diorama. Kids can also take pictures of their summer creations, like forts, outdoor theaters, or sculptures.

Together, make a scrapbook with photos, drawings, fun decals, stamps, postcards, maps, and original writings. Create interesting borders or feature pages. Keep a record of your child's baseball games; make a list of his favorite foods; save ticket stubs from an amusement park or from a trip on an airplane, train, or bus; collect maps from a subway, bike, or car trip; save menus, place mats, and coasters from favorite restaurants and

diners; draw pictures of the best and worst things that happened. Create pages over the summer, using postcards received and photos taken.

Summer Treasure Box

Help children design a box to store summer treasures like shells, postcards, baseball cards, handmade sculptures, audiovisual recordings of an event, restaurant menus and receipts, and ticket stubs and programs from performances and amusement parks. Include one or two books that your child read and especially enjoyed, or souvenirs from trips. You might even add the charts from this book after you have filled them out together.

Decorate treasure boxes with fabrics or wallpaper and with original art. When summer is over, suggest that children put together an exhibit for relatives and friends; exhibits could remain in the kids' bedrooms or the family room for a short time, perhaps making the transition back to school easier. It is fun, and also useful, to pull out a box of treasures in February to help start brainstorming for the upcoming summer.

Poster or Banner

Suggest that your children design a poster: "The Summer of 19__." To create a poster collage of memories, use photos, drawings, decals, news clippings, patterns of kites, pictures of familiar hiding places, and so on. Use strong shapes and colors for making posters. Try to use two or three different styles of lettering. Have a strong image with one central message in large letters; the rest can be in various sizes of smaller print.

Create summer images on a cloth banner, using markers, stencils, felt cutouts, embroidery, appliqués, patches, and other decorative materials. Add to the banner throughout the summer. Consider hanging the banner as an outdoor flag.

T-Shirt and Visor

Stencil "Fun Fabulous Summer" on T-shirts and visors. Get fabric markers or fabric paint so that children can decorate their caps and shirts with some of the best summer recollections. Kids will be proud of their work and have fun wearing it.

Letters

At the middle and end of the summer, while your memories are still fresh, you and your children should write letters to yourselves about the summer, its highlights, and its failures. Encourage children to say anything they want about themselves and their summer. What did they like the best about summer? What would they like to do next summer that they did or didn't do this summer? Have children put the letters in envelopes addressed to themselves. Mail the letters the next year when your family begins planning summer activities. Do the same yourself; write about what the summer meant to you.

These mementos of summer, with all its passions and surprises, will be a source of fun and enlightenment when you pull them out next year. If all goes well, come September, your children will be thrilled with the summer that's past and will look forward to the next one. As a parent, you will be able to look back and say, "That was a great summer! It was fun, it was exciting, and it was enjoyable. It was the best summer we've ever had."

Appendix

User-Friendly Tools

Your family can start right away having the best summer ever with these user-friendly tools. The *Yes, No, Maybe Chart* discussed in chapter 2 has been designed for your child to fill in (or try copying it for repeat use). Also, feel free to copy the *Family Message Center* and let your child paste it together on poster board (the example shown is just one way to do it). Other ideas to add to your *Family Message Center* might be Favorite Snacks to Make, Favorite Books and Magazines to Read, and Favorite Places to Go, or anything you and your child dream up. Why not start summertime planning *today?* Have fun!

YES, NO, MAYBE CHART

	YES	NO	MAYBE		YES	NO	MAYBE
1. Athletic Activities				Gymnastics			
Aerobics				Hiking			
Badminton				Horseback riding			
Baseball, softball				Horseshoes			
Basketball				Jogging			
Baton twirling				Juggling			
Bicycling				Jumping rope			
Boating				Kayaking			
Bowling				Kite flying			
Canoeing				Martial arts			
Cheerleading				Mountain climbing			
Croquet				Paddle tennis			
Fencing				Pool			
Field Hockey				Racquetball			
Fishing and fly-fishing				Roller-blading			
Football				Roller-skating			
Frisbee				Sailing			
Golf				Scuba diving and snorkeling			

	Yes	No	Maybe		Yes	No	Maybe
Self-defense				Candle making			
Skateboarding				Carpentry			
Soccer				Cartoon drawing			
Street hockey				Ceramics and pottery			
Surfing				Clockmaking			
Swimming				Computer graphics			
Tennis				Crocheting			
Track and field				Decoupage (collage)			
Water games				Designing, making posters			
Water-skiing, water sliding				Doll and dollhouse making			
White-water rafting				Doodle art			
Wrestling				Embroidery			
Yoga				Fabric painting			
				Flower arranging and pressing			
				Freehand drawing			

2. Cultural Activities

ARTS AND CRAFTS	Yes	No	Maybe		Yes	No	Maybe
Architectural design				Game making			
Batiking				Illustrating stories			
Cake decorating				Kaleidoscope making			
Calligraphy				Kite making			
				Knitting			

	Yes	No	Maybe
Macramé			
Mask making			
Model building			
Mural painting			
Needlepoint			
Oil painting			
Origami			
Papermaking and marbling			
Photography			
Printmaking			
Puppet making			
Puzzle making			
Quilting			
Rug making			
Sand sculpting and painting			
Sculpting			
Sewing			
Stained glass			
Stamping with rubber stamps			
Stenciling			
Tie-dyeing			

	Yes	No	Maybe
Watercolor			
Weaving			
Woodcraft and woodwork			
DANCE			
Ballet			
Ballroom dance			
Belly dance			
Creative movement			
Folk dance			
Jazz dance			
Modern dance			
Square dance			
Swing dance			
Tap dance			
DRAMA			
Acting and community theater			
Choral reading			
Clown lessons			
Costuming			
Face painting and make-up			

	Yes	No	Maybe
Improvisation			
Magic tricks and card tricks			
Mime			
Mysteries, creating, reading			
Play production and writing			
Prop making			
Puppetry and puppet making			
Set construction			
Storytelling			
Theater games			
Ventriloquism			

MUSIC

	Yes	No	Maybe
Band—concert, jazz, and marching			
Chamber music			
Chorus			
Composing			
Making instruments			
Music appreciation			
Song writing			
Voice lessons			

	Yes	No	Maybe
MUSICAL INSTRUMENT LESSONS			
Accordion			
Autoharp			
Bass			
Bassoon			
Cello			
Clarinet			
Cornet			
Cymbals			
Drums			
Flute			
Guitar			
Hand bells			
Harmonica			
Harpsichord			
Horn			
Keyboard			
Maracas			
Oboe			
Organ			

	Yes	No	Maybe
Piano			
Piccolo			
Recorder			
Saxophone			
Tambourine			
Triangle			
Trombone			
Trumpet			
Tuba			
Viola			
Violin			
Xylophone			

3. Community Activities

	Yes	No	Maybe
American Red Cross Programs			
Big Brothers/Big Sisters Association			
Boys Clubs and Girls Clubs of America			
Camp Fire, Inc.			
Collectors' clubs			

	Yes	No	Maybe
Community newspaper			
Community programs			
Computer clubs			
Educational groups (study of mammals, study of rocks)			
4-H programs			
Garden and nature groups			
Get a job			
Historical societies			
Hobby clubs			
Humane society (taking care of animals)			
Language clubs			
Library and reading clubs			
Parks and recreation program			
Religious activities			
Special needs organizations			
Sports/fitness programs			
Student exchange programs			
Student letter exchange (pen pals in another country)			

	Yes	No	Maybe
Summer theater groups			
Volunteer programs			
Writing clubs			
YMCA and YWCA			

4. Outdoor and Nature Activities

	Yes	No	Maybe
Animal farm or shelter—study the animals			
Archaeological program—attend and participate in a dig			
Astronomy—learn about the universe			
Audubon societies—join in a summer program or go on walks			
Backpacking—go on an adventure			
Beach—walking, building sand castles, and studying marine life			
Bird feeder—build one and record the birds			
Bird-watching			
Botanical gardens—explore and study			

	Yes	No	Maybe
Butterflies—observe			
Cranberry bog or blueberry farm— visit and study the process			
Farm—visit a few and compare the activities			
Forest and wood life—explore it			
Geology—collect, identify, and polish rocks			
Islands—visit one, study life on it, and sleep overnight			
Life on a river—study it			
Mountain climbing			
Natural history—join a club			
Nature centers—attend a local program and crafts class			
Outdoor survival skills			
Pond life—explore it			
Science—attend classes and workshops at museums and planetaria			
Trees, shrubs, and flowers— study and classify			

	Yes	No	Maybe
Whale watching			
Wild edible plants—classify			
Zoo—visit and study the animals			

5. Ideas to Spark Summer Interests

	Yes	No	Maybe
Animals—adopt and care for one			
Astrology—study the stars, moon, and sun			
Aviation—learn about planes and make flying things			
Bubbles—make a mixture and experiment			
Cars—study old and new models			
CB radio			
Chemistry—begin to experiment			
Collecting—baseball cards, coins, dolls, shells, or stamps			
Computers—learn new programs			
Cooking and nutrition			

	Yes	No	Maybe
Designing and writing—greeting cards, logos, and gift wrappings			
Entomology—study insects			
Experimenting with electricity			
Film—make home videos			
Finance—set up a bank account and keep track of spending			
Game playing—backgammon, card games, checkers, chess, Clue, cribbage, and Dungeons and Dragons			
Genealogy—study your family history or make a tree			
Geography—look at maps			
History—study a period you're interested in			
Humor—write jokes, tell riddles, read and draw comics			
Inventions—make new things			
Journalism—write newspaper stories, ad copy, and press releases			

	Yes	No	Maybe
Languages—learn spoken or sign languages			
Learn about different countries			
Magic—perform tricks			
Math games—solve problems			
Meditation			
Mind-stretchers and mind games			
Model car and plane construction			
Navigation—map out the next trip			
Outer space and UFOs			
Pets—training and grooming			
Plant a garden—vegetable, flower, or herb			
Puzzles—complete and frame			
Radio—short wave and Morse code			
Radio announcing, taping interviews, and doing productions			
Read books of your choice and keep a record of them			
Recycle at home			
Research your town and its activities			

	Yes	No	Maybe
Sea and ocean life—learn all about various fish			
Take a transportation ride just for fun—train, boat, plane			
Terrarium—make one			
Treats—make candy with molds, ice cream, cookies, no-bake snacks			
Write (books, newspapers, poems, plays, and folk tales)			

6. Fun Places to Go in the Summer

	Yes	No	Maybe
Airport			
Aquarium			
Bakery			
Band concert			
Beach			
Book publisher			
Bottling company			
Campsite			
Candle factory			

	Yes	No	Maybe		Yes	No	Maybe
Candy factory				Museum			
Car manufacturing plant				Music concert			
Circus				Nature reserve or zoo			
Clothing manufacturer				Parades			
Computer company or store				Parents' places of work			
Country fair				Parks—amusement, theme, water, or nature			
Courthouse or state capitol							
Dance recital				Planetarium			
Farmers' market				Political rally			
Fireworks display				Printing company			
Garage sale or flea market				Puppet show			
Greenhouse				Radio or TV station			
Historical site				River			
Hotel				Seaport			
Ice cream factory				Sports event			
Lake				Sugar factory			
Library				Telephone company			
Magic or juggling show				Theater or summer stock			
Movies				Top of the highest building			
				Toy manufacturer			

FAMILY MESSAGE CENTER

FAMILY SUMMER SAFETY RULES

- Jennifer to wear sunscreen at lake!
- Ride bike with helmet!
- Extra key is with Mrs. Wilson next door
- Only Ramona or Alison's mom can pick up Jennifer
- Fire drill this Saturday AM

FUN THINGS TO DO WHEN THERE'S NOTHING TO DO

Finish Grandpa's puzzle and your book
Practice new magic tricks for Friday's family night
Watch Aladdin and The Sound of Music again
Send cousin Amy a care package at camp

PHONE NUMBERS TO CALL

Father at Work	555-3845
Mother at Work	555-3799
Neighbor or Nearby Person	
Grandparent Special Relative	555-9004
Friend	555-2278
Operator	
Emergency Number	
Police Department	
Fire Department	
Family Doctor	
Ambulance	
Poison Control Center	
Other Important Numbers	

JENNIFER'S CALENDAR FOR: JULY

S	M	T	W	TH	F	S
		1 Go to Nature Camp with Alison at Willow Pond	**2**	**3**	**4**	**5**
6 Tea Party for Beatrix Potter's Birthday	**7** Send out invitations for Birth of the Ice Cream Cone party	**8** Ramona to sit	**9** Ramona to sit Go to arts and crafts	**10** Ramona to sit Go for a river cruise	**11** Ramona to sit Go to arts and crafts	**12** Ramona to sit
13	**14**	**15**	**16**	**17** Get camping stuff together	**18** Camping	**19** Camping
20 Camping	**21** Plan Wednesday's party	**22**	**23** Birth of the Ice Cream Cone party	**24** ?	**25** ?	**26** Go star-gazing with Dad
27	**28** Make Grandma's present— picture frame	**29** Grandma's birthday	**30**	**31** Register for soccer clinic!		

SUMMER RESPONSIBILITIES AND CHORES

Jennifer to do: Thursday

Mow lawn
Feed Chi-Chi
Change water in fish tank
Set table

CALENDAR FOR: _____

S	M	T	W	TH	F	S

PHONE NUMBERS TO CALL

Father at Work _____

Mother at Work _____

Neighbor or Nearby Person _____

Grandparent/Special Relative _____

Friend _____

Operator _____

Emergency Number _____

Police Department _____

Fire Department _____

Family Doctor _____

Ambulance _____

Poison Control Center _____

Other Important Numbers _____

_____

_____

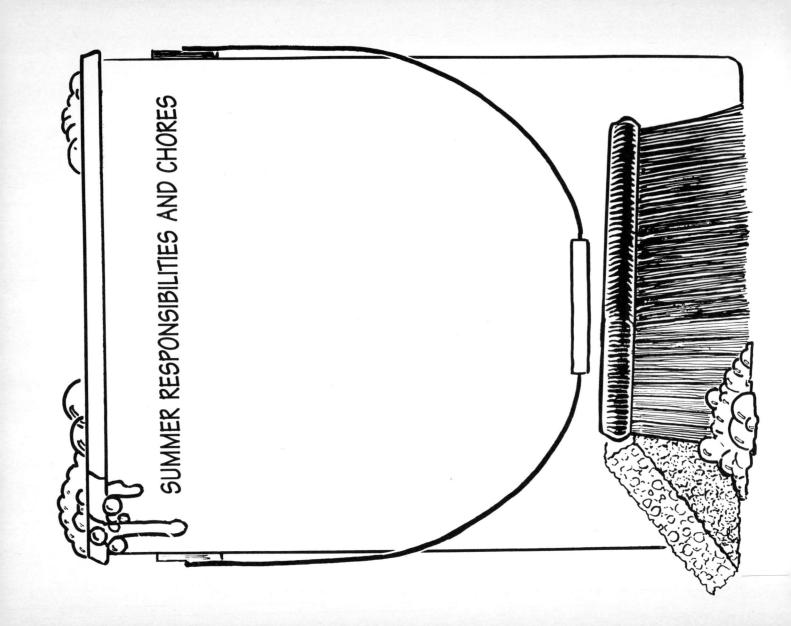

SUMMER RESPONSIBILITIES AND CHORES

FAMILY SUMMER SAFETY RULES

Resources

· · · · · · · · · · · · · · ·

SUMMER ACTIVITIES

Allison, Linda. *The Sierra Club Summer Book.* New York: Random House, 1994. Information on trips, crafts, activities, and games—all planned with concern for environmental protection.

Auerbach, Stevanne, Ph.D. *Dr. Toy's Smart Play: How to Raise a Child With a High P.Q. (Play Quotient).* New York: St. Martin's Press, 1998.

Bennett, Steve. *365 Outdoor Activities You Can Do with Your Child.* Holbrook, MA: Adams Media Corp., 1993. An array of projects that will delight parents and kids.

Bergstrom, Joan M., and Craig Bergstrom. *All the Best Contests for Kids,* 5th ed. Berkeley, CA: Ten Speed Press, 1995. A Parents' Choice winner and National Parenting Center Seal of Approval. Something for every kid: art to science to soapbox derbies and pancake flipping.

Blakey, Nancy. *The Mudpies Activity Book: Recipes for Invention.* Berkeley, CA: Ten Speed Press, 1995. An easy-to-follow guide to spontaneous creative activities.

Drake, Jane. *Kids' Summer Handbook.* New York: Ticknor & Fields, 1994. Books for Young Readers. Outdoor recreation, including nature crafts and handicrafts.

Gillis, Jennifer S. *Green Beans & Tambourines: Over 30 Summer Projects & Activities for Fun-Loving Kids.* Williamstown: Storey Communications, Incorporated, 1995.

Levine, Shar. *Einstein's Party Book: Simple Instructions for Spy Parties, Bubble Parties, and Much, Much More.* New York: John Wiley, 1993. How to put together clever, easy, and inexpensive theme parties for curious kids.

Marsh, Carole. *A Kid's Book of Smarts: How to Think, Make Decisions, Figure Things Out, Budget Your Time, Money, Plan Your Day, Week, Life & Other Things Adults Wish They'd Learned When They Were Kids!* Atlanta, GA: Gallopade Publishing Group, 1994.

Stackpole Books Staff. *Kid's Guide to Crafts Holiday Projects, Spring & Summer.* Harrisburg, PA: Stackpole Magazines, 1995.

Stautberg, Edward. *What Kids Like to Do.* Portland: MasterMedia, 1993. Innovative and entertaining ideas of activities and excursions for children of all ages.

Wallace, Edna. *Summer Sizzlers & Magic Mondays: School-Age Theme Activities.* Nashville, TN: School Age Notes, 1994.

Warner, Penny. *Kids' Holiday Fun: Great Family Activities Every Month of the Year.* Deephaven, MN: Meadowbrook, 1994. Ideas for holiday activities the whole family can enjoy.

SUMMER CAMPS

American Camping Association Staff. *Guide to Accredited Camps, 1997/98.* N. Martinsville, IN: ACA, 1997. This annual guide features special indexes that allow you to find a camp by activity, special need, special group, or location that meets the strict standards of the ACA. To order, call 800-426-CAMP.

Guide to Summer Camps and Summer Schools, 27th ed. Boston, MA: Porter Sargent, 1995. Current facts on more than eleven hundred recreational and educational summer opportunities—camps, schools, and specialized programs for people with physical, mental, or learning disabilities.

Kennedy, Richard. *Choosing the Right Camp,* 1995-96. New York: Random House, 1995. A complete guide to help you find the best summer camp for your child.

Marlor Press Editors. *My Camp Book: A Guide to Journaling Summer Camp Experiences for Kids Ages 8-15.* St. Paul, MN: Marlor Press, 1994.

Queen, Margaret M. *So You're Off to Summer Camp: A Trunk Load of Tips for a Fun-Filled Camp Adventure.* Nashville, TN: Foxglove Press, 1993.

Peterson's Summer Opportunities for Kids & Teenagers, 1998. 15th ed. Princeton, NJ: Peterson's Guides, 1998. All the information you need to find the perfect summer program or vacation for your child.

FAMILY VACATIONS

American Automobile Association Editorial Staff. *The AAA Guide to North America's Theme Parks*. 3rd edition. Heathrow, FL: AAA, 1997. One hundred of America's most popular theme parks.

American Automobile Association Editorial Staff. *AAA Travel Activity Book*. Heathrow, FL: AAA, 1990. A fun-filled book with questions and answers about every state in the country.

Best Hikes with Children. Series. Seattle, WA: Mountaineers, [various dates]. Available for many areas including Colorado, Connecticut, Massachusetts, New Jersey, New Mexico, Pennsylvania, Rhode Island, Utah, Vermont, and many more. Information on great family hikes.

Family Travel Times. New York: Travel With Your Children (TWYCH), a division of Dorothy Jordan and Associations. A magazine that regularly covers such topics as children's programs, travel books, family attractions, and worldwide family destinations.

Fodor's Travel Publications Staff. *The Complete Guide to America's National Parks, 1998-99*. New York: Fodor's Travel Publications Inc., 1997.

Fodor's Travel Publications Staff. *Great American Learning Vacations*. 2nd ed. New York: Fodor's Travel Publications Inc., 1997.

Foster, Lynne. *Take a Hike!* New York: Little, Brown & Company, 1991. The Sierra Club's beginner's guide to hiking and backpacking.

Kauffman, Liz. *The Highlights Book of Travel Games*. Honesdale: Boyds Mills Press, 1994. Games and puzzles to ponder, and adventures to imagine on portable game boards.

Kaye, Evelyn. *Family Travel: Terrific New Vacations for Today's Families*. Boulder, CO: Blue Panda, 1993. Complete details of where to find adventure and environmental trips, farm stays, house rentals and exchanges, rafting and canoeing trips, camping, hiking and biking, and more.

Kidding Around. Series. Santa Fe, NM: John Muir Publications. Available for destinations such as Atlanta, Boston, Hawaiian Islands, London, Los Angeles, New York City, San Francisco, and more. Designed to make the world more accessible to young travelers and help them find out what to do, where to go, and how to have fun when they are away from home.

Klutz Press Editors. *Kids Travel: A Backseat Survival Kit*. Palo Alto, CA: Klutz Press, 1994. An activity pad, felt pens, dice, string, a geography bee, palm-reading techniques, license plate bingo, a Parcheesi board and playing pieces, and more.

Knorr, Susan M. *Books on the Move: A Read-about-It, Go-There Guide to America's Best Family Destinations*. Minneapolis, MN: Free Spirit Publishing, Inc., 1993.

Murray, Beth. *Highlights Book of Travel Fun, Crafts & Activities for the Car, Plane, Bus, or Train*. Honesdale: Boyds Mills Press, 1995.

Norris, John. *Amusement Parks: An American Guidebook*. 2nd ed. Jefferson, NC: McFarland & Company, Inc. Publishers, 1994. A guide to amusement parks from coast to coast.

O'Brien, Tim. *Where the Animals Are: A Guide to the Best Zoos, Aquariums, & Wildlife Attractions in North America*. Chester, CT: Globe Pequot Press, 1992.

Rand McNally Staff. *Cool Places U.S.A.* Skokie, IL: Rand McNally, 1994. Games and puzzles relating to places kids love to visit such as cities or national parks.

Rand McNally Staff. *Kids' U.S. Road Atlas*. Skokie, IL: Rand McNally, 1996. The only state-by-state road atlas made especially for children with large-scale maps detailing highways, roads, and cities.

Rubin, Alan A. *The Complete Guide to America's National Parks, 1994-1995*. 6th ed., revised. Washington, DC: National Park Foundation, 1990.

Stapen, Candyce H. *Fifty Great Family Vacations*. Series. Old Saybrook, CT: Globe Pequot Press, [various dates]. Best family destinations including what to see and do, where to stay, and recommended day trips.

Sutherland, Laura. *Best Bargain Family Vacations, U.S.A.* New York: Saint Martin's Press, Inc. 1997. How to plan affordable and enjoyable family vacations.

Webster, Harriet. *Going Places: The Young Traveler's Guide & Activity Book*. New York: Simon & Schuster, 1991.

Whitefeather, Willy. *Willy Whitefeather's River Book for Kids*. Boulder, CO: Roberts Rinehart Publishers, Inc., 1994. Teaches river skills to kids.

Wiley, Kim W. *Walt Disney World with Kids. 1998 edition*. Rocklin, CA: Prima Publishing, 1997. Advice for avoiding long lines and saving time and money.

TOYS, BOOKS, SOFTWARE, VIDEOCASSETTES, AND VIDEO GAMES

Atkinson, Doug. *Videos for Kids: The Essential, Indispensable Parent's Guide to Children's Movies on Video*. Rocklin, CA: Prima Publishing, 1994. Includes complete descriptions of the action as well as notes on violent content, questions that young viewers may ask, themes, and so on.

Auerbach, Stevanne, Ph.D. (Dr. Toy). *Dr. Toy's Best Children's Vacation Products for 1997.* Dr. Toy is an expert in play, toys, children's products, education, parent education, child development, child care, and special education. Visit her web site: **http://www.drtoy.com** to find award winning toys, books, software, dolls, games, puzzles, CDs, audio and video CDs and tapes, creative materials, construction toys, and lots more.

Club KidSoft. Los Gatos, CA. A fun, educational, and inspirational magazine, CD, and on-line service that helps kids learn about computers. Web site: **http://www.kidsoft.com**

Deniz, Carla B. *Only the Best: The Annual Guide to the Highest Rated Educational Software & Multimedia.* Alexandria, VA: Association for Supervision & Curriculum Development, 1997. An up-to-date annual guide to the newest educational programs that have won distinction.

Donavin, Denise P. *American Library Association Best of the Best for Children: Software, Books, Magazines, and Videos.* New York: Random House, 1992. Librarians' recommendations for books, magazines, videos, audio, software, toys, and travel.

Ginn, Karen H. *Taming the Electronic Babysitter: A Guide to Children's Videos for Parents & Caregivers.* Louisville, KY: Bridge Resources, 1996.

Green, Diana H. *Parents' Choice: A Sourcebook of the Very Best Products to Educate, Inform, and Entertain Children of All Ages.* Kansas City, MO: Andrews & McMeel, 1993.

The Latest & Best of the Educational Software Selector (TESS), 1993 edition. Hampton Bays, New York: Educational Products Information Exchange Institute, 1993. A compilation of educational programs currently on the market for Macintosh and DOS.

Levine, Evan. *Kids Pick the Best Videos for Kids.* New York: Carol Publishing Group, 1994. Hundreds of movie, cartoon, how-to, educational, and sports videos rated by kids.

Liggett, Twila C. *The Reading Rainbow Guide to Children's Books: The 101 Best Titles.* New York: Carol Publishing Group, 1994. The best titles selected from more than 400 children's books broadcast on PBS.

Oppenheim, Joanne and Stephanie. *Best Toys, Books, Videos for Kids 1998: Oppenheim Toy Portfolio.* Rocklin, CA: Prima Publishing, 1997. A guide to kid-tested classic and new products for ages zero to ten.

Perkins, Michael C. *KidWare: A Parent's Guide.* New York: T.A.B Books, 1994. An invaluable reference covering the best choices of software for children ages three to thirteen.

Turck, Mary C. *A Parent's Guide to the Best Children's Videos & Where to Find Them.* Boston, MA: Houghton Mifflin Company, 1994. A concise volume to help parents select and critique more than two hundred videos based on gender roles, violence, language, and cultural diversity.

SUMMER SAFETY – Books and Videocassettes

Boelts, Maribeth. *A Kid's Guide to Staying Safe on the Streets.* The Kids' Library of Personal Safety Series. New York: Rosen Publishing Group's PowerKids Press, 1997. Discusses ways children can be safe around strangers, traffic, and other potentially dangerous situations.

Chaiet, Donna. *The Safe Zone: A Kid's Guide to Personal Safety.* New York: William Morrow, 1998.

Fancher, Vivian Kramer. *Safe Kids: A Complete Child-Safety Handbook and Resource Guide for Parents.* New York: Wiley, 1991.

Glaser, Nily. *Be Street Smart—Be Safe: Raising Safety Minded Children.* Riverside: Gan Publishing, 1994.

Grollman, Earl A. *Teaching Your Child to Be Home Alone.* New York: Free Press, 1992. A resource guide for parents and children.

Gutman, Bill. *Be Aware of Danger.* Focus on Safety Series. New York: Henry Holt, 1996. Discusses how to deal safely with strangers and dangerous situations in school and on the streets.

Kasdin, Karin. *Disaster Blaster: A Kid's Guide to Being Home Alone.* New York: Avon, 1996. A guide to staying home alone that offers practical advice on caring for younger siblings, staying on top of accidents, calling for the correct assistance when needed, and handling emergencies.

Korem, Dan. *Streetwise Parents, & Foolproof Kids.* 3rd ed. Richardson, TX: International Focus Press, 1998. Invaluable lessons for kids & adults.

Merry, Wayne. *Official Wilderness First-Aid Guide.* Toronto, Canada: McClelland & Stewart/Tundra Books, 1994. Information about situations that children and adults may face in the outdoors.

Smith, Becky J. *Is It Safe?: Injury Prevention for Young Children.* Santa Cruz, CA: E.T.R. Associates, 1994. Information and tips for building safe environments for young children. Includes strategies for preventing injury and ways to control the extent of trauma if an injury does occur. Call 800-321-4407.

Statman, Paula. *On the Safe Side: Teach Your Child to Be Safe, Strong, and Street-Smart.* New York: HarperCollins, 1995. A busy parent's guide to teaching everyday safety skills to school-aged children.

Struber, Robert. *Smart Parents, Safe Kids: Everything You Need to Protect Your Family in the Modern World.* Kansas City, MO: Andrews and McMeel, 1997. Includes information about online safety and crime prevention.

Weiner, Florence. *Kids Home Alone: Ready to Be Home Alone.* New York: Safety Center, 1997.

SUMMER SAFETY – Organizations and Programs

AMERICAN CANCER SOCIETY, INC., 1599 Clifton Road, NE, Atlanta, GA 30329-4251. The ACS supports numerous public and professional education programs, including curricula for public schools. Web site: **http://www.cancer.org**

AMERICAN HEART ASSOCIATION. Check the phone book for your local affiliate. The American Heart Association is a national voluntary health agency whose mission is to reduce disability and death from cardiovascular diseases and stroke. Web site: **http://www.americanheart.org**

AMERICAN RED CROSS, 431 18th Street, NW, Washington, DC 20006-5310. The Red Cross teaches CPR, first aid, water safety, and AIDS awareness; provides counseling; and is guardian of the nation's largest blood bank. Web site: **http://www.redcross.org**

BICYCLE HELMET SAFETY INSTITUTE, 4611 Seventh Street South, Arlington, VA 22204-1419. A consumer-funded program that acts as a clearinghouse and a technical resource for bicycle helmet information. Web site: **http://www.bhsi.org/**

JR. FIRE INSPECTOR PROGRAM sponsored by First Alert, Inc., 3901 Liberty Street Road, Aurora, IL 60504. Helps local fire departments teach young children the basics of fire safety through educational programs and fun activities. Call 630-851-7330 or visit their web site: **http://www.firstalert.com/jr_fire_inspector.html**

THE KIDS ON THE WEB: SAFETY ON THE NET. This is a web site with information about a variety of software packages available to try to help keep children safer on the Internet. Web site: **http://www.zen.org/~brendan/kids-safe.html**

KIDS TEACHING KIDS PROGRAM sponsored by the Minnesota Highway Safety Center, St. Cloud State University, 720 Fourth Avenue South, St. Cloud, MN 56301-4498. Their goal is to help kids prepare early, first as passengers, then as drivers. Call 320-255-4733 or visit their web site: **http://www.stcloudstate.edu/~mhsc/ktk.html**

NATIONAL CAMPAIGN TEACHES KIDS TO BE AIR BAG SAFE, National Association of Governors' Highway Safety Representatives, 750 First Street, NE, Suite 720, Washington, DC 20002-4241. "The ABCs of Air Bag Safety—The Back is Where It's At" is a nationwide campaign that provides valuable free information to help keep children safe in vehicles equipped with air bags. Web site: **http://www.naghsr.org**

NATIONAL CRIME PREVENTION COUNCIL, 605 East Government Street, Pensacola, FL 32501. An organization founded to prevent crime and build safer, more caring communities. McGruff and Scruff the Crime Dogs are crime prevention symbols of the National Citizens' Crime Prevention Campaign. The NCPC also sponsors youth programs such as Youth as Resources (YAR) and Teens, Crime, and the Community (TCC). Web site: **http://www.ncpc.org**

NATIONAL PARENT TEACHERS ASSOCIATION, 330 N. Wabash Street, Suite 2100, Chicago, IL 60611-3690. PTA activities include work in various areas of child health and safety such as encouraging traffic safety education and establishing nationwide projects on smoking and health, seat belt and child restraints, and AIDS education. Call 312-670-6782 or visit their web site: **http://www.pta.org**

NATIONAL PROGRAM FOR PLAYGROUND SAFETY, School of HPELS, University of Northern Iowa, Cedar Falls, IA 50614-0618. The latest information on playground safety and injury prevention. Call 800-554-PLAY or visit their web site: **http://www.uni.edu/playground**

NATIONAL SAFE KIDS CAMPAIGN, 1301 Pennsylvania Avenue, NW, Suite 1000, Washington, DC 20004-1707. The Safe Kids Buckle Up program promotes correct car seat and safety belt usage. Check out their web site for the "Family Safety Checklist" to see how your family measures up. Call 202-662-0600 or visit their web site: **http://www.safekids.org**

NATIONAL SAFETY COUNCIL, 1121 Spring Lake Drive, Ithasca, IL 60143-3201. The Youth Activities Division of the National Safety Council provides activities and opportunities for the development of good health and safe living behavior leading to the prevention of youth injuries and death. Call 708-285-1121 or visit their web site: **http://www.nsc.org/mem/youth.htm**

U.S. CONSUMER PRODUCT SAFETY COMMISSION, Washington, DC 20207. Information about the latest safety tips to prevent injuries, product recalls, including bicycle and baseball safety, in-line roller skating and skateboard hazards, kids speaking out on bike helmets, baby sitting tips, and more. Call 800-638-2772 or visit their web site just for kids: **http://www.cpsc.gov/kids/kids.html**

Index

THE ACTIVITIES CLUB®

Appeal to a Child's Sense of Curiosity, Exploration, and Fun!

The Activities Club® is an innovative program that introduces children ages 6-12 to exciting hobbies and helps them to develop lifelong interests.

Adds Excitement to School-Age Programs

Make The Activities Club a foundation for your school-age program. The ideas and materials guarantee that children will explore, discover, invent, and experiment for hours! The Activities Club offers Theme Guides and Resource Packages for groups of children, which are perfect for all types of school-age programs, such as: Before and After School, Vacation and Holiday, Year-Round Intersession, and Camp.

Helps End Boredom at Home

In 1996, The Activities Club introduced an award-winning line of Hobby Kits for children to explore at home. As seen on *Good Morning America,* these individual kits contain several hands-on projects and self-directed experiments. Each kit is designed to promote hours of invention, fun, and experimentation. The Hobby Kits were chosen as one of *Dr. Toy's Ten Best Creative Products* in 1995 and 1996, and for *Dr. Toy's Best Vacation Products* in 1997.

Explore These Exciting Themes

With The Activities Club, school-age children can explore exciting themes such as:

Welcome to the Club!	Marvelous Masks
Soaring with Birds	Nature's Treasures
Cool Running Clocks	Papermaking with Pizzazz
Creative Cooking	Photography in a Snap!
Take Flight!	Sensational Sea Life
Gads of Games	Stamping Safari
Awesome Gifts!	Blast Off to the Universe!
Gold Medal Games	The Homework and
Wacky Inventions	Edutainment Club
Presto! It's Magic!	

Here's What People Are Saying About The Activities Club:

". . . fun, exciting, and educational! The sense of ownership that kids get with The Club fosters creativity, independence, and responsibility."

—EMPLOYEES' CENTER FOR YOUNG CHILDREN, INC

"Constructive, fun, and bedazzling projects."

—THE BOSTON GLOB

"The ideas are wonderful! The [children] are having a great time!"

—KINDERCAR

For information about The Activities Club for your school-age program or for your child, call (800) 873-5487 or go to **http://www.activitiesclub.com**